FACILITATING
PROJECT PERFORMANCE
IMPROVEMENT

FACILITATING PROJECT PERFORMANCE IMPROVEMENT

A Practical Guide to Multi-Level Learning

Dr. Jerry Julian

HarperCollins
LEADERSHIP

AN IMPRINT OF HARPERCOLLINS

ADVISORY BOARD

Bill Gardner has worldwide responsibility for Executive Assessment, Executive & Leadership Development, Succession Planning, Learning & Collaborative Technologies, Performance Management, Corporate Learning & Development, and Organization Development for Advanced Micro Devices (AMD). Under Bill's leadership AMD's Learning & Development organization was named to *Training* magazine's Top 100 learning and education groups in 2001, 2002, 2003, and 2004. He holds a B.S. in Finance from Mississippi State and an M.B.A. from the University of Southern Mississippi.

Dave Medrano is an Associate Dean for the corporate university of one of the world's leading multinational automotive companies where he directs training and development to support sales and marketing functions. He is also responsible for reconfiguring training programs for the company's global workforce. He speaks internationally to industry groups and holds a B.A. from the University of California at Los Angeles and an M.B.A. from Pepperdine University.

Rich Wellins, Ph.D., is a Senior Vice President with Development Dimensions International (DDI) where his responsibilities include leading the Center for Applied Behavioral Research, developing and launching a new leadership development system, and building systems for internal knowledge management. He is a frequent speaker and has written six books, including the best seller *Empowered Teams*. He holds a Doctorate in social/industrial psychology from American University.

CONTENTS

FOREWORD

Project work in many organizations today is "the new normal." An up side to project work is the opportunity for rich learning. Project teams form a temporary community with a common focus even though members may be spread around the world and often cross professional, functional, and cultural boundaries. Project teams bring people together with diverse backgrounds to achieve shared aims on common tasks under tight time-lines—often in collaboration with customers and other stakeholders —in ways that require innovation and knowledge sharing.

However, the conditions under which project teams work are challenging and turbulent, and organizations are not always prepared to change the way they work when they become "projectized." Learning in project teams often requires coordination, alignment, and intentionality. Team members learn by experimenting and using results to adjust their plans and processes as they work.

But many project teams are not able to learn quickly in ways that not only help them complete projects on time and under budget but that also build knowledge, skills, and improvements for team members, project groups, and the larger organization. And even when project teams do learn, these insights, approaches, and competencies are not mined by the organization to benefit work of other project teams.

Jerry Julian describes these difficult learning conditions as "red light learning" and proceeds to show how an organization can instead engage "green light learning." This book will help readers who want to accelerate project team learning and find ways to leverage that learning across boundaries within the organization. Julian introduces a multi-level learning framework in which project and program managers can put reflection into practical use before, during, and after work cycles. He introduces a common framework and shows how it can be used differently to (1) improve continuous learning and innovation *within teams*, (2) strengthen effective process improvement *across teams*, and (3) engage strategic learning at the portfolio management level *across the organization*.

Julian's multi-level learning model is based on principles of lean manufacturing, agile development, continuous improvement, reflective learning from and through experience aimed at overcoming defensive routines, communities of practice, and team and organizational learning. These principles include (1) satisfying the customer, (2) eliminating waste, (3) welcoming new insights, (4) delivering as fast as possible, (5) empowering team learning, (6) seeing the whole, (7) using a third-party coach, and (8) reflecting at multiple levels. Julian infuses this multi-level learning model with insights from interviews with 20 Project Management Office leaders and six project managers from a variety of functional disciplines. He also describes the new role of the multi-level learning coach in some detail in Chapter 3 to help those who assume these functions better support their organizations in moving toward an adaptive, continuous system-level learning approach.

As contributing editors, we hope you will appreciate this addition to the Adult Learning Theory and Practice book series. We seek to showcase practical frameworks, tools, and perspectives that you—as leaders and facilitators of learning in organizations—can use with some confidence because they are not just the latest fad, but are based on solid, research-based understanding combined with the wisdom of experience. Some books in the series emphasize structured learning approaches, e.g., training, education, and development in classrooms and new virtual meeting and learning places. This book showcases learning-in-action that takes place on the ground, integrated with work, and in less formal ways (though perhaps intentional and designed). We are interested in supporting learning for individuals, but also collective learning sustained in groups, communities of practice or interest, and organizations.

We hope you enjoy and benefit from this volume, and we look forward to your feedback and thoughts on other topics in this series.

Victoria J. Marsick

FACILITATING PROJECT PERFORMANCE IMPROVEMENT

INTRODUCTION

Does your or your organization's success depend on the ability to deliver successful projects? Are you interested in helping project teams, project managers, and senior executives improve their ability to execute mission-critical projects and programs? If you answered yes to both of these questions, then this book is for you. It provides a practical guide to facilitating business transformation and performance improvement for project organizations that's grounded in cutting-edge research in the fields of project management and organizational learning. The goal is to equip you, the reader, with the knowledge, skills, and tools that will enable you to engage people and teams in a process of continuous learning, innovation, and performance improvement. The goal is to ensure success in the implementation of new organizational strategies, the development of new products, the rollout of new systems, and the management of mission-critical programs. Multi-level learning is an approach that focuses on helping organizations deliver rapid results, learn, and deliver again, providing value to customers, eliminating waste, and delivering increasing levels of value as projects and programs proceed through their life cycle.

By deploying the techniques and practices in this book, you will be positioned to help your project organization:

- Reduce time to market for new products, systems, processes, and technologies.
- Improve customer and end-user satisfaction with project outcomes.
- Reduce the risk of failure, wasted investment, and runaway projects.

1

- Improve productivity, quality, and teamwork.
- Continuously improve delivery from one project, phase, or iteration to the next.

Let's face it, project environments require learning on the job. Every new project requires project managers and teams to plan out their approach, even if it's only slightly different from the one they used the last time. Every new project and every phase of every project presents new challenges and opportunities. There aren't always established routines for solving every problem or seizing every opportunity that surfaces on a project. Moreover, organizational priorities can change and markets can shift while projects are "in flight." Thus, every stage of every project or program provides new experiences that require managers and teams to learn, adjust, and take action. As a result, project organizations need mechanisms that enable them to continually adapt to ensure that they are focused on the right projects at the right time, that their processes are agile and effective, and that project teams are continually innovating from one phase to the next and from one project to the next.

There are companies that have found great value in combining the concepts of lean operations with structured learning and reflection to deliver faster results that enable them to transform and continuously improve. They've built these practices into their ongoing project and program management approach. Agile software development practices are breaking new ground on this front. These approaches engage team members in structured retrospectives after each iteration (lasting from a few days to a few weeks). The retrospective focuses on what's working, what's not working, and what needs to improve for the next iteration. The U.S. Army has been using a similar approach in its training of combat teams in the deserts of California (Darling, Parry, and Moore, 2005). Units huddle after simulated battles to reflect on the original intent, what actually happened, and what can be improved for the next battle. The insights are then spread around the world to fight new enemies, who are themselves adapting to changing conditions. The computer chip maker Intel has adopted the use of retrospectives to improve its product development practices around the globe (Lavell and Martinelli, 2008a). Retrospectives have been so successful there that the company now has more than 65 people who are trained to conduct these sessions on a regular basis, leading to improvements not just on a single program, but on others that can use the innovations to improve quality and reduce development time.

Clearly, reflection is not just for philosophers, poets, and academics. It has been built into the way work gets done to improve performance in some of the best learning organizations in the world.

Yet while many organizations have adopted high-performing learning practices, structured reflection most often occurs in a postproject review or "lessons-learned" session at the end of a project—if it happens at all. Intel and many other companies have found that this practice isn't working. By the time the session takes place, it is often too late to allow teams to improve, and the team members may not remember everything that happened over the course of a multimonth or multiyear program. The result is that structured learning and improvement are deferred until it's too late—or avoided altogether. Because of this, learning remains informal and incidental in most project organizations, and, as we shall see later, this type of learning creates undesirable surprises, blowups, and embarrassments for senior managers and teams alike.

Organizations simply cannot afford to leave learning to chance on their mission-critical investments. That's because without mechanisms for systematic learning, problems continue to remain under the surface, perhaps without being addressed at all, until they snowball into larger issues that trigger a "red light" on the project status reporting system (Julian, 2008). Monumental failures can occur, leaving a wake of damaged reputations, blame, and losses of both time and money for the organization.

Leaving learning to chance not only can lead to outright failures, but has huge opportunity costs. Improvements that could shorten project delivery time, improve productivity, reduce cost, or improve quality can go unexploited and forgotten. As a result, the organization winds up spending countless more time, dollars, and personnel on future projects. In the extreme, each project team reinvents the wheel every time it starts a new project. It is even more likely that this will happen in environments with poor cross-project communication and stressed-out project managers and teams.

MULTI-LEVEL LEARNING: AN APPROACH TO IMPROVING PROJECT AND PROGRAM PERFORMANCE

Multi-level learning helps to overcome many of the problems that project organizations face. It helps to reduce risk, deliver faster results, eliminate waste, and improve teamwork on mission-critical efforts. Its focus is on facilitating systematic reflection at three levels: strategies, processes, and projects. In larger organizations, these levels of learning may also reflect levels of the organization. Senior teams may be primarily responsible for developing strategy and structuring a portfolio of projects and programs that will enable the organization to carry out that strategy. Program managers or project management office (PMO) leaders may be charged with sharing practice knowledge across projects to streamline processes, reduce waste, and shorten delivery time. And project teams may be charged with the primary responsibility for achieving objectives that deliver results for external and internal customers (to distinguish internal from external customers, in the rest of this book, the former will be called *internal clients*). In multi-level learning, teams at each of these levels are empowered to take primary responsibility for their own learning. And if you've worked in project-intensive environments, you know how important it is to engage teams at all levels in order to effect meaningful improvement. After all, decisions made at each level affect the others. Achieving business transformation success means not only delivering successful projects, but also selecting the right projects to begin with. It also means supporting teams by providing approaches and methodologies that help them carry out their work in the most effective way.

Multi-level learning is a closed-loop system that directs actionable feedback to the way work gets done at each of these levels. It is not just bottom-up nor top-down; it is both. Nor is it an end in itself. It is a vehicle for achieving the organization's strategic goals, for transforming the way in which business gets done, and for generating better outcomes on mission-critical projects and programs, from one phase to the next and from one project to the next.

Figure I.1 shows the multi-level learning framework. Beginning with Level 1, project teams are the core driver of innovation, learning, and improvement. The focus at this level is on continually innovating and improving projects as they progress, not just reflecting at the end to develop "lessons learned" that get stored in databases and don't get used. Instead, project teams stop and reflect at regular intervals while the project is in flight so that they can define improvements and tangible action items that can be actively applied during the next phase. The result is learning and performance improvement as the project progresses, reducing the risk of project failure, improving team effectiveness, and providing real-time feedback and development opportunities for project members.

In Level 2 of the multi-level learning framework (the cross-project improvement level), project managers are enlisted, perhaps by a project or program management office, to improve processes that span multiple projects and programs. At this level, project managers team up and tackle specific cross-project problems and opportunities that, when adequately addressed, will improve delivery effectiveness across the many projects in the portfolio, creating a "multiplier" effect. Process improvement is at the core of this approach, in which project managers actively reflect on mission-critical organizational processes, develop specific strategies for improving these processes, and test and validate these strategies as projects progress in order to implement improvements that break down bureaucracy, reduce waste, eliminate delays, and unlock innovation. This kind of improvement process is much more powerful and practical than simply hosting knowledge-sharing sessions or reporting lessons learned among project managers. The result is real improvement across projects and buy-in from those who need to implement the change. Engaging project managers to improve cross-project processes can reduce costs, improve productivity, and cut down on the time required to deliver results.

At Level 3 of the multi-level learning framework, senior managers and sponsors play a pivotal role. Their decisions about strategy and project selection have wide-ranging implications for the organization. Therefore, they themselves also engage in periodic reflection on the organization's overall project portfolio and its ability to achieve the organization's strategy. Rather than focusing on a specific project, the strategy retrospective is focused on broader programs and strategies, of which projects are only a part. Questions include: Are the projects in the pipeline enabling the organization to achieve its intended strategy? What adjustments need to be made to ensure that we achieve our intended results? Which projects need to be initiated, cancelled, or repurposed? What actions need to be taken, and at which levels of the organization?

FIGURE I.1
The Multi-Level Learning Framework

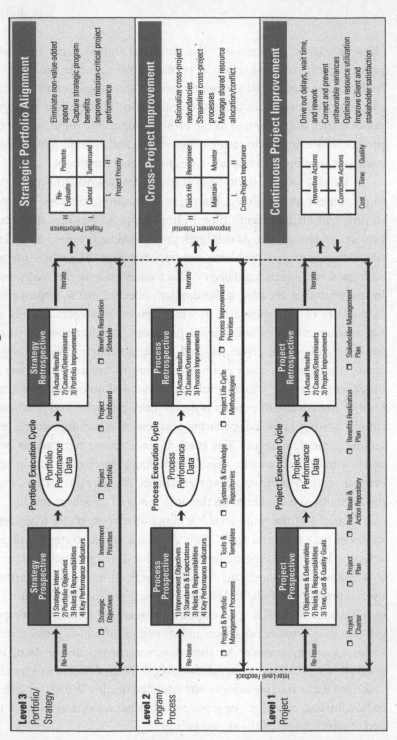

Learning at all three of these levels is a necessary and critical principle of multi-level learning. Underpinning the learning at each are individuals who learn collectively on behalf of the organization. It is individuals and teams who press their talents into service in solving the organization's most critical challenges. And it is individuals and teams who are able to learn, adapt, and improve, carrying out work that meets the needs of customers and key stakeholders. Each of the three levels of multi-level learning provides individuals and teams with opportunities for reflection on not only the content of problems, but the processes by which these problems get solved, as well as whether or not the right problems are being addressed in the first place. Through these levels of learning, individuals give and receive feedback that, when facilitated by a multi-level learning coach, can lead to high-impact professional development and performance improvement for the organization overall.

You may be wondering by now about the overhead required for this approach. Does this mean that the organization will require a dramatic cultural shift in order to make it work? The answer to this question is no. Multi-level learning can be viewed as an "add-on" to a firm's existing project management approach and organizational routines. If anything, multi-level learning helps to streamline, synchronize, and accelerate work, not add unnecessary processes. Effective multi-level learning provides members of the organization with the structures and space that they need if they are to learn, reflect, and improve effectively—even if this is not already part of the organization's cultural fabric. If these practices are effectively introduced into the organization, and if senior managers believe in their benefits, then it's possible, and maybe even likely, that a culture change will emerge as a result of continued deployment. But such a change is not a requirement for the introduction of multi-level learning. The most critical requirement is a willingness to learn and improve. If there's a will, then this book can help to show you the way.

HOW THIS APPROACH DIFFERS
FROM CONVENTIONAL APPROACHES

Many of the conventional approaches to improving project performance that have been advocated by software vendors, standards bodies, and professional associations focus on improving "project management maturity"—deploying external standards and best practices, implementing new project management software, or conducting formal training programs. All of these approaches may be useful, yet they either downplay or ignore altogether the knowledge, wisdom, and experience that are already resident in the organization and can be cost-effectively applied to improving performance within and between projects. What's missing from these approaches is a systematic method of facilitating learning from project experience so that the organization can focus its own talents and capabilities on solving and preventing problems and improving performance—and doing so in a way that works for the organization's unique culture and needs rather than imposing outside standards that require large amounts of training or consulting dollars to be effectively deployed.

PROJECT AND PROGRAM MANAGEMENT OFFICES

Many project organizations have also implemented a project or program management office to improve project performance. While a PMO can be a highly effective mechanism for facilitating performance improvement, most PMOs consider learning opportunities to be those situations in which a team or project manager didn't follow the established procedures. Deviations from the methodology often become the only learning experiences that the PMO recognizes. Because of this, PMOs are often perceived as an extra layer of management that simply creates bureaucracy and more rules that bog down projects. The result is often a contentious relationship between teams and the PMO, one that creates rigidity and political wrangling that limits performance gains, inhibits innovation and learning, and saps morale.

While many PMOs, they can also play an invaluable role in facilitating learning and performance improvement if they are structured and operated in an adaptive way. Chapter 2 provides a road map for PMOs that want to become more effective in this role.

HOW THIS BOOK CAN HELP YOU
AND YOUR ORGANIZATION

The purpose of this book is to help you, the reader, effectively deploy and facilitate multi-level learning to improve project performance in your or your client's organization. Its primary objective is to help managers and facilitators enhance the learning process as work occurs, so that more projects succeed and the organization improves in a measurable way. This book provides a model, a set of tools, and applicable theory that can help you facilitate continuous improvements in project performance both within and across projects.

Those who have the courage and the desire to facilitate learning from project experience should read on. And you should know that you're in good company, among both researchers and practitioners in the fields of project management and organizational learning. Many organizations have found great value in the tools and techniques described in this book and have built them into their ongoing project management routines, as we will see in later chapters.

WHO SHOULD READ THIS BOOK

This book is written primarily for executives, managers, and facilitators in project organizations, including information technology, product development, consulting, research and development, research and advisory, and a myriad of other organizations that depend on projects to achieve their strategic objectives. This book will be helpful to:

- Executives who want to improve their organization's ability to deliver new strategies and projects more effectively and reliably
- Project management office leaders who want to learn about a cost-effective way to improve project, process, and portfolio performance
- Organization development practitioners, facilitators, and consultants who want specific approaches and tools to help teams and individuals learn from project experience to improve their performance and develop their talents
- Project managers who wish to improve their team's performance,

improve collaboration, and solve risks and issues as they occur, before they mushroom into larger problems

HOW THIS BOOK IS ORGANIZED

This book is organized in three parts: foundations, roles, and implementation. Part 1 covers the origins and principles of multi-level learning. Chapter 1 discusses the problems found in many project organizations, including the reasons why informal and incidental learning can lead to blowups and surprises, and how multi-level learning overcomes these challenges by providing mechanisms for continuous systems-level learning. Chapter 2 provides an overview of the foundations and principles of multi-level learning, drawing on both research in organizational learning and cutting-edge practices in the fields of operations improvement and software development.

Part 2 covers the roles required to deploy multi-level learning. Chapter 3 provides an in-depth discussion of the role of the multi-level learning coach—an objective, third-party learning coach who helps teams reflect, learn, and continually improve at three levels: project, process, and the overall project portfolio. It describes models of how the multi-level learning coach can help teams at each of these levels deliver rapid results and continually innovate from one stage or iteration to the next. It covers approaches by which the multi-level learning coach intervenes to facilitate effective communication, problem solving, decision making, conflict resolution, and boundary management when dysfunctional group processes limit the ability of teams to reflect productively. Chapter 4 covers the role of the program management office and how the leaders of such a group (and others who serve in a similar cross-project role) can serve as knowledge brokers who connect communities of practice, including project teams, senior management, and other functional groups, so that they can continually improve. As PMO leaders are the "glue" that binds together the levels of the multi-level learning approach, the chapter also provides recommendations for how they can become more effective in this role.

Part 3 provides step-by-step instructions for facilitating multi-level learning at each of three levels: project, process, and strategy. Chapter 5 provides the reader with an understanding of how to plan and facilitate project-level learning and performance improvement as projects progress, reducing the risk of project failure, improving team effectiveness, and providing real-time feedback and development opportunities for project members.

Chapter 6 discusses how to engage project managers and key subject-matter experts in the development and implementation of improvements that cross multiple projects. While project teams can solve many problems while they are in flight by engaging in retrospectives, there are some problems or opportunities that affect multiple projects, and their solutions may be beyond the scope of a specific project team. These challenges are actively addressed at the cross-project improvement level.

Chapter 7 provides the reader with an explanation of how to facilitate multi-level learning with senior teams to ensure alignment between the project portfolio and the organization's strategy. Senior managers play a pivotal role in the multi-level learning process. They engage in periodic reflection on the organization's overall project portfolio—those projects that are in progress, those that are complete, and those that are planned to start in upcoming periods—to ensure that it is structured in a way that achieves the organization's strategic objectives.

For those readers who are interested in additional theory and research, Appendix A presents a discussion of why traditional "lessons-learned" practices aren't effective in enabling ongoing performance improvement.

Appendix B covers theories of situated learning and communities of practice, an understanding of which helps to highlight the challenges that PMO leaders and teams face in working across organizational boundaries to effect learning and change.

PART 1

Foundations

1 | THE NEED FOR MULTI-LEVEL LEARNING

Projects are the vehicle for transforming the modern global corporation. They are the means by which businesses achieve leaner cost structures, more effective operations, and better IT. They are the means by which companies develop new products and execute new business strategies. When projects succeed, they deliver revenue growth, improved productivity, lower costs, more efficient operations, and higher market valuations. When they fail, they drain critical investment dollars, waste valuable resources, and—directly or indirectly—limit a firm's ability to compete.

While projects are vital to organizational growth, renewal, and success, project work is fraught with uncertainty, risk, and ever-changing internal and external conditions. Every project and each phase of every project presents new problems and challenges that require managers and teams to plan, act, and adjust. Organizational priorities may change as new managers rotate into and out of roles. External economic conditions may change, making some projects more urgent and eliminating the need for others altogether. Requirements for new products or software applications may change in midstream as customers and stakeholders learn more about what they really need. Mergers and acquisitions, divestitures, joint ventures, and new strategic initiatives create discontinuities and place new demands on the organization and its top talent, drawing away resources at critical times (Dai, 2002).

In addition to navigating a changing social and political landscape, people at all levels must increasingly learn to work with new people, new technologies, and new business processes across different time zones, cultures, and functional disciplines as work becomes more geographically distributed.

Not only do project organizations face the challenge of changing internal and external conditions, but they are under pressure to continually improve performance, increase productivity, reduce costs, and trim timelines from one phase of a project to the next and from one project to the next. This is especially true for organizations that generate revenue solely from the delivery of projects and programs to external customers, such as those firms in the outsourcing, consulting, engineering, software development, and construction industries. However, it is increasingly true for internal groups such as information technology, product development, research and development, marketing, and operations.

The problem is that for many project organizations, systematic learning primarily happens either after a project is concluded or after major problems have occurred, when the damage has already been done. Take, for example, the experience of a major high-tech medical device manufacturer. The company lost millions on a massive project that required multiple business units to coordinate their efforts for a single customer installation. Time delays, rework, cost overruns, and contractual penalties ultimately combined to produce a monumental failure that the company's executives wanted explained and remedied. Ed, the leader of the project management office (PMO), launched a postproject review and asked the team to develop a case study with recommendations for future projects. A few days later, the PMO received a call from someone in sales: "Ed, we've got a project that's going off the rails over here. We need your help." Ed realized that the project she was talking about had all the hallmarks of the previous failure. Within 24 hours, the management team put the case study recommendations into action and avoided millions more in potential cost overruns and penalties.

There is good news and bad news in this story. The good news is that the organization found that performing a project retrospective (also often called a postproject review, project postmortem, or after-action review) had tremendous value. Performing the retrospective and documenting the results through a case study probably saved the company millions more in future project failures. After all, projects often share the same organizational environment, including common tools, people, and processes. This means that improvements on one project can improve other projects, saving the organization time and money while preventing future losses and dissatisfied customers.

The bad news is that the company was unable to prevent the problems before the losses accrued, despite the existence of a regular project review process by the PMO. The net result is that it cost millions for the company to learn a hard lesson. And it doesn't have to be that way.

RED-LIGHT LEARNING

When project organizations do not have effective mechanisms for learning, it remains largely informal and incidental, embedded in the everyday work routines of organizational members and happening largely unconsciously (Marsick & Watkins, 2001). Improvement, innovation, and problem solving are often left to chance. Issues may go unaddressed or avoided, creating abrupt surprises, blowups, or "fire drills" that trigger a red light on the "traffic light" reporting system for project status (Julian, 2008a). In these situations, project teams are hastily assembled so that senior managers can find out what went wrong; this creates an environment riven by political infighting, threats to individuals' jobs and career prospects, "blamestorming," and avoidance of the "truth" for fear of reprisals by managers or peers. The result is that people at all levels actively avoid reflection, largely because it is perceived as being too threatening, political, ineffective, or all of the above. This creates a self-reinforcing cycle, because when structured reflection is avoided, the result is further opportunities for blowups and surprises. This "red-light learning cycle" is depicted in Figure 1.1.

When people and teams are thrust into these red-light learning situations, both the people involved and the organization lose. There are several reasons why red-light learning can be harmful to long-term performance. First, under these conditions, the underlying root causes of problems may never be discovered or adequately addressed. Peers will hesitate to speak about one another's performance for fear of throwing their colleagues "under the bus" in the presence of managers. Channels of communication become blocked, muted, or distorted, and the analysis that does occur often winds up being directed at outside parties, such as vendors or other departments. This means that the true root causes may never be found, leaving the problems unsolved.

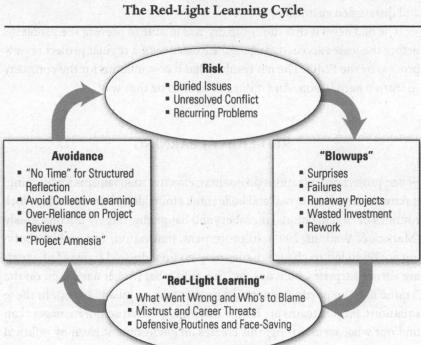

FIGURE 1.1
The Red-Light Learning Cycle

Second, under red-light learning conditions, a team's potential to reach high levels of performance and collaboration can be severely diminished. The need to "search for the guilty" can often create animosity, conflict, or communication barriers that persist into the future, inhibiting organizational effectiveness. And regardless of economic conditions, the most talented individuals may either "check out" or leave altogether. This may not be the kind of place you or your best people want to work.

The third reason that red-light learning is detrimental to project organizations is related to how people perceive the process of "learning." The fallout from red-light learning in the form of animosity, distrust, and unresolved conflict can mean that project team members may avoid involvement with future "lessons-learned" sessions altogether, knowing not only that these sessions can strain relations with colleagues, but that the real root causes may not be adequately addressed. What this adds up to is that learning from project experience can be perceived as a waste of time by employees and managers alike.

It may be no surprise, then, that previous researchers have noted "time pressures" as a significant barrier to learning from past project experiences (Disterer, 2002; Keegan & Turner, 2001; Schindler & Eppler, 2003; Zedtwitz, 2003). In A. Keegan and J. R. Turner's study of 19 project-based firms, for example, the authors found that it was "common throughout the study for respondents to list impressive practices in place to facilitate organizational learning, and then at the very end to state they do not work, or are not used, because of the time pressures on those people whose learning is the focus of these systems" (p. 91).

DEFENSIVE ROUTINES

Indeed, it may not be simply a lack of time that limits systematic learning, but rather defensive routines that arise from red-light learning. Chris Argyris (1995) describes organizational defensive routines as "any action, policy, or practice that prevents organizational participants from experiencing embarrassment or threat and, at the same time, prevents them from discovering the causes of the embarrassment or threat" (pp. 20–22). "Face-saving" is one such defensive routine, the rules of which Argyris describes as follows: "When encountering embarrassment or threat, bypass it and cover up the bypass."

Other researchers have found the symptoms of defensive routines in a number of studies, often taking the form of project members' fear of publicly airing mistakes or pointing the finger at other team members (Disterer, 2002; Prencipe & Tell, 2001; Schindler & Eppler, 2003; Zedtwitz, 2003). In interviews of 27 R&D managers from 13 multinational companies, for example, Maximilian Zedtwitz (2002) found that public feedback among team members in postproject reviews is "softened and rendered ineffective" for the sake of smooth cooperation among staff members on future projects. Moreover, he found that project members also feared acknowledging issues related to their own performance that might be considered mistakes or failures for fear of embarrassment or threat to their career.

Take, for example, the experience of Melissa, the leader of a PMO who observed a "lessons-learned" session with a project team:

> The project manager was just absolutely despised because of his approach. [He was] a nice guy, but his approach was always attacking people. So unfortunately that's what that turned out to be . . . that attitude still came through and it was sort of a blame environment, even though we tried very much not to [have it that way].

She then went on to talk about how a more senior manager attending the meeting used "time pressures" as a way to focus solely on what went wrong:

> And it was really interesting because the director who was in there said, "Do you know what? We don't have time. This is a short meeting. Let's not worry about what went well. Let's just focus on what went wrong."

It is perhaps not surprising that time pressures were also given as the reason why the findings were never distributed, communicated, or acted upon:

> By the time he came back, he said, "Well, yeah. That's great feedback, but I really don't have time." And it never went out to anyone. I don't think the feedback went to anyone, in the end. . . . We're setting up the PMO but there's not a lot I can do about this one, only in thinking about the whole postmortem process in general.

Under conditions of red-light learning, which may also include heated lessons-learned sessions as in the example just given, learning and reflection can become perceived as being a punitive experience, making it more likely that defensive routines will be perpetuated, further reducing the utility and effectiveness of these sessions with teams in the future.

The presence of defensive routines may also explain the reasons that project reviews don't always bring problems to the surface until it's too late. Because project reviews are "top-down"—that is, their purpose is to inform management of the status of a project and obtain approval to move forward—problems may not be brought up for fear of reprisal, embarrassment, or threat. In other words, defensive routines may conspire to undermine the learning process in project reviews, often making them an ineffective mechanism for teams to solve problems effectively. Moreover, project reviews catch problems largely after they occur, when there are variances from project timelines, budgets, and expectations. By the time problems reach the radar screen of the PMO or senior management, much of the damage may already have been done. It is usually much more expensive to fix the problems once they've created delays, frustration, or rework.

Having explored the problems associated with ineffective learning practices in project organizations, we now turn to what the conventional wisdom has taught us about learning from project experience and why these traditional approaches have proven ineffective in the real world of project work.

PROBLEMS WITH TRADITIONAL APPROACHES TO LEARNING FROM PROJECT EXPERIENCE

By far the most pervasive technique for learning from project experience touted by academics, researchers, and professional associations is the practice of identifying and documenting "lessons learned" at the end of each project so that these "lessons" can then be transferred to future project activities (Julian, 2008b). The roots of this practice reach as far back as the 1980s, when Gulliver (1987) wrote a seminal article titled "Post Project Appraisals Pay" in the *Harvard Business Review*, describing British Petroleum's approach to learning from one project to the next. He states that the sole mission of the postproject appraisal process is "to help British Petroleum worldwide learn from its mistakes and repeat its successes" (p. 128). The process involved investigating the original intent of each project and whether or not that intent was carried out effectively.

Conducting lessons-learned sessions—also called postproject reviews, after-action reviews, project postmortems, and debriefings—is now a popular standard in project management practice (Bresnen et al., 2003; Disterer, 2002; Kotnour, 2000; Prencipe & Tell, 2001; Zedtwitz, 2003). Project management guidelines established by the Project Management Institute currently call for lessons learned to be captured and retained after each project is completed (Project Management Institute, 2004). Maximilian Zedtwitz (2002) claims that postproject reviews are "one of the most structured and most widely applicable approaches to passing on experience from one team to the next" (p. 256).

These "lessons-learned" practices involve project members in reflective discussions about what went well and what went wrong, with the aim of improving future project performance (Kotnour & Vergopia, 2005; Zedtwitz, 2002). The resulting lessons are then documented and stored in databases or on corporate intranets for retrieval by future project teams (Kotnour, 2000; Newell et al., 2006).

While these practices have become standard in project management guidelines, the research shows a very bleak state of affairs with respect to their deployment and efficacy. Lessons learned are not always documented, and even when they are, they most often go unused (Antoni et al., 2005; Bresnen et al., 2003; Keegan & Turner, 2001; Newell, 2004; Newell et al., 2006; Prencipe & Tell, 2001). Moreover, organizational members express clear dissatisfaction with the process (Keegan & Turner, 2001).

In a survey completed by 62 managers from the United States, Europe, and Japan representing more than 20 R&D organizations, Zedtwitz (2003) found that 80 percent of all projects were not reviewed at all after completion, and the remaining 20 percent were reviewed without the use of a formally structured process.

Martin Schindler and Martin Eppler (2003) conducted action learning research with nine multinational companies and also found that there is a "great discrepancy" between the need for project debriefing and its actual deployment in practice. Additionally, in a review of several empirical studies conducted in IT project environments, George Disterer (2002) notes, "Project information is rarely captured, retained, or indexed so that people external to the project can retrieve and apply it to future tasks."

In a study of 19 firms in project-based industries, Anne Keegan and J. Rodney Turner (2001) found that all the companies in their study, "without exception," had lessons-learned policies in place to capture learning from projects once they were completed. Yet even though there were policies in place to hold the reviews, they rarely happened. Worse, the authors found that "in no single company did respondents express satisfaction with this process" (p. 90). Sue Newell et al. (2006) claim that "we need to consider problems with the actual practice" of lessons learned.

There are three fundamental problems associated with the lessons-learned approach that render it largely ineffective. First, it defers structured learning from experience until the end of a project, perhaps months or even years after the project began. Project team members can easily forget the problems that arose, having dealt with them and perhaps solved them weeks or months earlier. By the time the lessons-learned session is conducted, the learning has become a distant memory—and that's if collective learning even happened in the first place. Perhaps the most damaging aspect of deferring structured reflection until the end of a project is people's lack of motivation for addressing the real issues. By the time the project is over, nothing can be done to resolve the problems that occurred. Team members may very well decide that addressing difficult conflicts or bringing up past problems is simply not worth it because it would serve only to open old wounds. They may feel that it's better to preserve working relationships among those in their organization than to jeopardize them for a project that's already completed. The desire to maintain harmony may very well outweigh the risks of dredging up the past when nothing can be done to fix the problem. Yes, there is the opportunity to help future teams, but that may not be a compelling enough motivation.

The second fundamental flaw associated with the lessons-learned approach is that it encourages learning from experience only at the project team level. In reality, projects are embedded within a constellation of communities of practice in the organization, getting demands, pressures, support, and guidance from many different sources—almost always from senior managers, from the program managers or the PMO (if one exists), and from other functional units within and outside the organization, including customers and key stakeholders. It may be unfair to have project teams be the only source of lessons learned, as this may imply that they are also the primary source of any problems that occurred. Senior managers and PMO leaders alike have much to learn from project experience. It could be argued, for example, that since these higher management levels launch and direct a multitude of projects, learning at those levels is even more important for the organization's overall health and performance.

It may be no wonder that some project teams consider structured learning from project experience a waste of time. After all, even if they do identify problems that need to be fixed the next time around, it may be the PMO and the senior managers who need to make the required changes, and if they are not part of the learning process, they may not understand the context or have the motivation to carry through with the team's input. They may even be threatened by the prospect of being perceived as part of the problem, choosing instead to focus on other issues that are less threatening. As a result, it may be that neither managers nor teams do anything to fix the problems for the next time around, creating a sense of frustration and futility that undermines future attempts at learning from project experience.

The third problem with lessons-learned practices is the assumption that people can learn effectively from "lessons" stored on databases. For those readers who are interested in some of the more theoretical aspects of the problems and opportunities associated with these practices, including why codification in databases has its limits, see Appendix A. It provides additional insights on this topic, particularly for those who are interested in knowledge management.

FROM RED-LIGHT LEARNING TO CONTINUOUS SYSTEMS-LEVEL LEARNING

Multi-level learning helps organizations overcome many of these challenges, including both the detrimental effects of red-light learning and the ineffectiveness of traditional lessons-learned and postproject review practices. It improves overall performance by expanding structured learning beyond the project team, increasing the quality and frequency of reflective practice, and providing more motivation for teams to learn in order to improve future performance. Multi-level learning expands learning beyond the project team by encouraging reflection at three levels simultaneously: projects, the processes that are common to multiple projects, and the overall project portfolio itself. These levels mirror the three types of reflection described by Jack Mezirow (1991) and include content, process, and premise reflection, each of which is discussed in more detail in Chapter 2.

The quality of learning is dramatically enhanced by the introduction of the multi-level learning coach, a skilled, objective, and substantively neutral third-party facilitator who helps teams learn and reflect more productively in ways that eliminate the potential bias associated with someone who has directed or influenced team decisions in the past. Chapter 3 discusses this role in more detail.

The frequency of reflection is increased by holding regular retrospectives throughout a project or program's life cycle, not just at the end. This enables teams to learn from the more recent past, when the memories, emotions, and experiences are still fresh in their minds. The improvements that emerge from these discussions are more robust, realistic, and effective in solving critical challenges.

It is because of the combination of these factors—expanded levels, better quality, and increased frequency of reflection—that teams are more motivated to engage in conscious learning from experience. Rather than going through an exercise aimed at documenting "lessons" for future initiatives, teams are able to identify actions that can solve their immediate problems and improve results at a time when something can still be done. Moreover, as a result of more frequent structured learning, team members become more adept at reflecting collectively in a group format, enabling them to feel more competent and skillful in the art of addressing sensitive issues and communicating in ways that reduce the impact of defensive routines, blame, and avoidance.

In addition to enhancing reflective practice in these ways, multi-level learning taps the knowledge-brokering role of the project or program management office. The PMO leader or program director who oversees multiple projects finds ways to build the improvements into the way work gets done on future projects and programs. Such leaders diffuse knowledge and maintain connections across multiple communities of practice, including senior management, project teams, and other functional disciplines. By doing so, they bring learning from retrospectives to the systems level, incorporating it into work routines, systems, methodologies, tools, and templates.

CONCLUSION

Victoria Marsick and Karen Watkins (1999) claim that in order for organizations to continuously improve, they must engage in continuous systems-level learning. Their view is based on the work of Chris Argyris and

Donald Schön (1996), who view organizational learning as occurring if two criteria are satisfied: (1) individuals, either appointed by management or anointed by followers, "take their learning back to the system," and (2) the system has "structures, processes and a culture in place to embed and support organizational learning" (Marsick & Watkins, 1999, p. 12).

By providing the people, practices, and mechanisms for continuous systems-level learning, multi-level learning prevents and mitigates surprises, delays, and blowups before they snowball into larger issues that trigger red lights. And it provides organizations with a means for proactively improving and developing individual talent simultaneously, opening new channels for effective communication and feedback and reducing the effects of performance-limiting defensive routines.

In the next chapter, we discuss the foundations and principles of multi-level learning, and how they help reduce waste, satisfy the customer, and leverage scarce resources more effectively in ways that improve overall organizational performance.

FOUNDATIONS AND PRINCIPLES OF MULTI-LEVEL LEARNING

In the last chapter, we discussed how informal and incidental learning in project organizations can lead to surprises and blowups that trigger red-light learning, resulting in "blamestorming" and other detrimental long-term effects. We also discussed the problems associated with traditional "lessons-learned" practices and why they have proved ineffective for facilitating learning and performance improvement—primarily because these practices defer structured reflection until after projects are over, when it is too late for teams to implement meaningful improvements. In this chapter, we discuss the foundations and principles of multi-level learning, beginning with the concepts associated with productive reflection, then moving to a discussion of how both the U.S. Army and companies adopting agile software development approaches engage in periodic reflection to improve performance from one iteration, one phase, and one project to the next. The chapter concludes with an overview of the principles of multi-level learning.

REFLECTION ON ACTION

In his book *Educating the Reflective Practitioner*, Donald A. Schön (1990) demonstrates how reflection plays an important role in the development of "professional artistry," the "kinds of competences practitioners sometimes display in unique, uncertain, and conflicted situations of practice" (p. 22). He distinguishes this type of competence from competence that is based solely on the application of the explicit rules and guidelines of one's profession. Professional artistry, according to Schön, involves the application of tacit knowledge, described by Michael Polanyi (1967) as that which we know but cannot readily express in words.

Despite the tacit nature of our "knowing-in-action," as displayed publicly through physical performances, Schön claims that "it is sometimes possible, by observing and reflecting on our actions, to make a description of the tacit knowing implicit in [these actions]" (pp. 25–28).

Schön's view of the reflection process begins when the application of our know-how does not produce the expected results, and we are surprised that our actions have failed to meet our expectations. After experiencing such a surprise, we may ignore it, or we may respond to it by reflecting in one of two ways. We may reflect on action by stepping away from the action and thinking back on our experience to understand how our knowing-in-action contributed to an unexpected outcome. Alternatively, we may "reflect in the midst of action without interrupting it." Schön refers to the former as "reflecting on action" and the latter as "reflection-in-action."

When we reflect, we question the assumptions behind our knowing-in-action and "think critically about the thinking that got us into this fix or this opportunity; and we may, in the process, restructure strategies of action, understandings of phenomena, or ways of framing problems."

Like Schön, Jack Mezirow (1991) defines reflection as a process whereby we "stop and think" about what we do or have done in order to "interpret and give meaning to an experience" (p. 104). He defines three types of reflection based on the object of the reflection process itself: content, process, and premise reflection. The first, content reflection, involves reviewing how ideas have been applied in solving problems at each stage of the problem-solving process. The second form of reflection, process reflection, examines the problem-solving process itself, focusing on the procedures and assumptions involved in previous applications. The third form of reflection, premise reflection, goes one step further by uncovering the assumptions that guided the need to address the problem in the first place.

Peter Cressey, David Boud, and Peter Docherty (2006) position reflection as a means of enhancing informal learning among communities of practitioners in the workplace. They claim that the application of reflection at work had previously been "the province of vocational training practitioners and discussed in terms of the training of individuals in the workforce" (p. 9). Yet two factors have created greater recognition of the need for productive reflection. First, informal learning has come to be recognized as a vitally important aspect of workplace learning. It has moved beyond its traditional role as a means of preparing professionals for the workforce and into the province of ongoing executive development through practices such as action learning, which was originally conceived by Reginald W. Revans (1971). The authors claim that this is because "issues of competence development cannot now be seen as separated from organizational and workplace practice" (Cressey et al., p. 12). The second factor influencing the increased recognition of the need for reflection in the workplace has been the organizational learning movement of the 1990s, in which group reflection is viewed as a cornerstone of organizational learning.

"Productive reflection," as defined by Cressey et al., has six key features. First, its outcomes are focused on the organization rather than the individual; it is collective rather than individual in its orientation. In the author's words, "productive reflection as we express it is focused on reflection to lead to action with and for others and for the benefit of the organization as well as the participants" (pp. 20–22). The second feature of productive reflection is that it takes place within the work environment and connects learning and work. In this view, work drives the reflection and frames what is legitimate. The third feature of productive reflection is that it can involve stakeholders at all levels, seeking to connect these stakeholders rather than isolate them within their own perspectives. Fourth, productive reflection is generative rather than instrumental in its focus. By this, the authors mean that productive reflection cannot be controlled in a way that leads to predetermined outcomes. It is exploratory and generative and cannot be reduced to "just another technique." The fifth feature is that productive reflection is developmental in character. It "is part of a range of organizational practices designed simultaneously to contribute to solving [the] organizational problems of today while equipping members of the organization to be better able to deal with challenges that face them in the future." The sixth and final feature of productive reflection, according to the authors, is that it is an open, unpredictable process that is dynamic and changes over time. That is, it is not possible to predict in advance where productive reflection will lead, and therefore it necessarily has unintended consequences. Moreover, productive reflection practices may change over time from one stage to another within the same environment, depending on the circumstances and the context.

THE U.S. ARMY'S AFTER-ACTION REVIEW PROCESS

If you think productive reflection is useful only for philosophers, academics, and poets, think again. Marilyn Darling, Charles Parry, and Joseph Moore (2005) describe the U.S. Army's approach to improving combat performance: the After Action Review (AAR). This program, developed and implemented by the U.S. Army, is now used in part by companies such as Colgate-Palmolive, DTE Energy, Harley-Davidson, and J. M. Huber. AARs are part of a planning and learning cycle that starts before and continues through simulated battles in the deserts of California. The cycle begins with a plan, drafted by a senior commander of the "opposing force," that includes the task to be completed, the purpose of the task, the commander's intent, and the expected result. These orders are then shared with subordinate commanders, who, through a "brief-back," verbally explain their understanding of the order. A rehearsal of the battle is then conducted to ensure that each unit has a clear understanding of its battle plan.

Darling et al. claim that this "before-action planning" helps establish the basis and climate for the After Action Review meeting, which occurs immediately following each phase of the battle. Subordinates clarify their orders in advance because they know that they will be participating in an AAR meeting after the event and will have to publicly discuss what worked and what did not.

The AAR meeting is most often facilitated by the unit leader's executive officer, the second in command. The meeting begins with "a reiteration of the house rules," which include: "Participate. No thin skins. Leave your stripes at the door. Take notes. Focus on our issues, not the issues of those above us [in the hierarchy]" (p. 88). The executive officer reiterates the original mission, intent, and expected outcome. The officer then describes the actual outcome, provides a brief review of events, and reviews associated battlefield metrics that relate to the original objective.

AARs focus on improving a unit's own learning and performance. Four questions are addressed in the AAR meeting: What was the intent? What actually happened? What caused the results? What will we sustain or improve? After the AAR is completed, Army leaders are "accountable for taking lessons from one situation and applying them to others—for forging explicit links between past experience and future performance" (p. 91).

The lessons learned in the desert battle simulations are often transferred by commanders to battlefields around the world. The Army is thus able to continually adapt and transform itself both on and off the battlefield to meet new global challenges and threats. The parallels for project organizations are clear: Before- and after-action reviews can provide the mechanisms needed to systematically learn from experience, enabling teams and project organizations to continually adapt to new challenges, adjust to changing conditions, and improve their performance.

Victoria Marsick and Karen Watkins (1999) reaffirm the importance of before- and after-action reviews in the corporate setting, claiming that they can enhance the informal learning of participants engaged in field experiences through "systematic reflection and structured intervention." It is through these processes of public reflection, they claim, that learning can be "shared and moved to a collective level of understanding" (p. 76).

Consistent with Marsick and Watkins's perspective on the importance of reflection for learning from experience, Joseph Raelin (2001) claims that public reflection is the key to "unlocking the learning" from project activities. Like Marsick and Watkins, Raelin claims that structured intervention must be provided in order to promote deeper levels of reflection.

THE EMERGENCE OF AGILE SOFTWARE
DEVELOPMENT PRACTICES

It's not only the U.S. Army, Colgate-Palmolive, DTE Energy, Harley-Davidson, and J. M. Huber that depend on the benefits that can be achieved from structured learning and reflection on team experiences. More and more software development organizations are utilizing agile software development practices to develop working software quickly and reliably under continually changing conditions. According to one estimate, 14 percent of North American and European enterprises were using agile-related methodologies in 2005, and another 19 percent were interested in deploying them in the future (DeJong, 2006).

Agile development is a team-based approach to satisfying the customer through frequent iterations of working software, each of which provides incremental benefit to the business, with earlier iterations providing the highest value. Central to agile approaches, including Scrum (Schwaber, 2004), is the project team retrospective, which is conducted at the end of each iteration and engages teams in reflection on the last iteration so that they can improve for the next one. Developed in 2001 by a group of software development consultants, the Agile Manifesto (Beck et al., 2001) consists of a number of key principles that differentiate agile development from traditional software project management approaches. The last of these principles lays the foundation for making the project retrospective a routine part of project work: "At regular intervals, the team reflects on how to become more effective, then tunes and adjusts its behavior accordingly."

Although there is no one agile "methodology," Scrum was developed in the 1990s by Ken Schwaber, one of the originators of the Agile Manifesto. Its purpose is to coordinate the activities of agile project teams (Schwaber, 2004). Scrum is a term coined by Hirotaka Takeuchi and Ikujir O. Nonaka (1986) to describe the "hyperproductive" product development practices they observed in Japanese and U.S. companies. Scrum refers to the strategy that rugby teams use to get out-of-play balls back into play by passing the ball within a team, moving as a unit bit by bit up the field.

Projects using the Scrum methodology employ multiple iterations to deliver working software that customers can use. After one or more iterations, a final product is released for implementation. This approach is a break from the traditional "waterfall" approach of developing software, in which the first step is to gather all requirements; the system is then designed, coded, and finally tested, all in a sequential manner. After months or sometimes years, the new software is released for implementation in the customer environment. As a result, traditional software development approaches view changes in requirements unfavorably, as the requirements must be "frozen" for the system to be developed in its entirety. Agile approaches, on the other hand, recognize that not all requirements can be completely known and specified up front. It recognizes that customers and stakeholders learn more about what they actually need as projects unfold. Moreover, agile recognizes that planning projects in detail up front is often mere speculation, not a deterministic process that results in a series of predictable activities that must be carried out long after the plan was developed. In reality, project plans evolve as conditions change and more becomes known about how to deal with the challenges at hand. By using frequent short-duration iterations, the team can plan a few days or weeks ahead, then reflect on its performance while that performance is still fresh in everyone's minds.

In Scrum, at the beginning of each iteration, or "sprint," the team sits down with the product owner for a sprint planning meeting. The product owner is responsible for representing the customer's needs and priorities and often provides the funding for the project. In the first part of the meeting, she lays out the vision for what the product is expected to do and how it should perform. The team then clarifies the content, purpose, meaning, and intentions of the product owner's vision and develops an associated list of product requirements. The team then determines what it can deliver in the upcoming iteration and commits to doing its best to meet that forecast. In the second half of the sprint planning meeting, the team plans the activities required to complete its work for the next iteration. These activities are then placed in a "sprint backlog" that incorporates all the team's expected tasks. The backlog evolves over the course of the iteration as work gets done and more detailed requirements become clear.

At the end of the iteration, the team holds a sprint review meeting. In this meeting, the team presents what was developed over the course of the iteration to the product owner and other key stakeholders. They provide feedback on the results and determine what the team should do next. After the sprint review meeting, the Scrum master facilitates a three-hour project retrospective, in which the team looks back on its work and identifies improvements that it can incorporate into its work for the next iteration.

Agile enables teams to learn from experience faster and more effectively by planning, delivering, and reflecting on small, incremental deliveries of project work, all the while getting feedback from customers and key stakeholders to ensure that the product meets their needs. Agile and Scrum enable teams to adapt to changing conditions, learning from one iteration to the next to improve their effectiveness. It is no wonder that so many organizations are adopting these practices and putting them to work to improve the way they deliver software.

ACTION-REFLECTION CYCLES:
THE FOUNDATION FOR MULTI-LEVEL LEARNING

Common to both the U.S. Army's After Action Review and agile software development are two critical events: a before-action review to ensure that everyone knows what to do, and an after-action review to reflect on what was actually accomplished and how it can be improved for the next time. These action-reflection cycles are the foundation of multi-level learning, and their usefulness is not limited to simulated battles and software development.

Intel, for example, conducts regular retrospectives over the course of product development projects to trim development time, reduce the risk of blowups and surprises, and spread the resulting learnings to other initiatives (Lavell & Martinelli, 2008c). Intel views retrospectives as a "ritual" in which team members get together over the course of a project or program's life cycle to reinforce what is working and identify what needs to be improved. Debra Lavell and Russ Martinelli (2008a) claim that this approach to improving projects while they are "in flight" is much more effective than the traditional practice of conducting postproject reviews or postproject audits. These traditional practices, they say, are held too late for any corrections to be made and have a negative connotation at the company as a result. Team members often don't want to show up for these traditional postproject reviews because they are perceived to be blame-oriented and nonproductive. Teams at Intel, they explain, learn best when they are solving immediate problems.

Rather than being facilitated by the project or program manager, as often happens with postproject reviews, retrospectives are facilitated by a trained, objective facilitator from outside the project team who helps draw people out to share their perspectives, creating an environment of safety rather than one of finger-pointing, defensiveness, avoidance, or blame. The benefits of retrospectives include improvement in project and program management practices, solving immediate problems through the rapid application of learnings, better odds of generating sustainable behavior changes, and improved team satisfaction with results through the use of a trained, objective facilitator.

Prospectives and retrospectives at regular points during a project's life cycle are at the heart of multi-level learning. We now turn to a discussion of its core principles.

PRINCIPLES OF MULTI-LEVEL LEARNING

In their book *Lean Software Development: An Agile Toolkit*, Mary and Tom Poppendieck (2003) describe the concepts and tools of lean development, and how they underpin the thought process and practices of agile software development. These principles have been put to work in the automotive industry since the 1970s, when Japanese automakers demonstrated the benefits that can be achieved through the application of these principles to manufacturing and production as well as to engineering and product development. Lean techniques enabled Japanese automakers to reduce their engineering effort by half, and enabled them to shorten product development time by a third. According to Jim Highsmith (1999), lean product development influenced his work in the development of Adaptive Software Development, which is also considered to be one of a number of approaches that are included in the agile software development family.

The principles of multi-level learning build on those of lean and agile (Poppendieck & Poppendieck), yet they include some important modifications and additions that are aimed at enhancing the learning process for the project organization overall. These principles include satisfy the customer, eliminate waste, welcome new insights, deliver as fast as possible, empower team learning, see the whole, use a third-party coach, and reflect at multiple levels. A brief description of each of these principles follows.

Satisfy the Customer

Multi-level learning focuses on ensuring that the outputs from project team activities are focused on delivering value to customers, whether those customers are internal or external to the organization. For organizations that provide project services directly to external customers, assessing customer satisfaction may be more straightforward, although not always easy. Many project organizations, however, provide project services to internal customers. For example, IT may develop new software and systems for the call center, or a Six Sigma group may perform projects that help the HR group. The HR group, in turn, may perform projects for the operations group. As stated in the Introduction, to separate internal customers from external customers in this book, we refer to internal customers as internal clients. In all cases, wherever this is feasible and possible, providing value to the external customer is always the goal. However, assessing internal client satisfaction with the external customer in mind may be the most practical approach for some projects. For example, a senior executive team may launch a project to develop a management reporting system that provides real-time performance reporting for key business activities. In this case, the customers are the management team members who need to use the resulting reports, as they are the primary judge of whether the reporting system meets their needs. The customer for this project is an internal client. When there is confusion over who the customer is for a given project, it is helpful for the organization to clarify who must use or implement the outputs from the project, as these people should be engaged routinely throughout the project to ensure that their needs are being met.

Eliminate Waste

Waste is any activity or component that does not ultimately add value for the customer. In manufacturing environments, waste can be unnecessary movement of materials, storing excess inventory, or making defective products that don't work. In project environments, waste includes unnecessary processes and bureaucracy that bog down teams and their innovative potential, project tasks and activities that do not contribute to achieving a project's objectives, and features and functions that customers do not perceive as useful or necessary. It also includes investments in projects or programs that don't help the organization achieve its strategic objectives. Not all waste can be completely eliminated, but the goal of multi-level learning is to eliminate as much waste as is possible and practical in order to get the job done to the customer's satisfaction.

Welcome New Insights

As discussed in Chapter 1, internal and external conditions continually change as teams define and implement strategies, and as projects progress through their life cycle. Traditional project management and "waterfall" development approaches tend to shun the introduction of change. Certainly, changes require updates to strategies, rescoping of projects, and upgrades to individual skill sets. This creates the potential for frustration and extra work. Yet if project organizations do not account for continually shifting conditions, they run the risk of developing irrelevant products, improving business processes that are no longer vital to the organization's competitiveness, or releasing software that doesn't meet the needs of customers. Change requires learning and adaptation. Yet welcoming it is preferable to continuing to squander scarce resources on projects, products, or processes that don't meet the needs of customers and stakeholders.

Deliver as Fast as Possible

Long cycle times for projects create opportunities for waste. Long delivery cycles mean that by the time a project delivers something, what it delivers may no longer be relevant or useful to the customer who requested it. Building in short cycles that produce tangible results for internal or external customers helps teams build momentum, learn from experience, and avoid wasteful spending. Moreover, delivering as quickly as possible enables project benefits to be captured sooner. For new product introductions, delivering faster means capturing new revenue sooner, preempting competitors with new innovations, and learning about what works and what doesn't so that the organization can maintain its edge in the marketplace.

Empower Team Learning

Teams are asked to take responsibility for their results, whether they are senior management teams developing strategy or project teams delivering software. In multi-level learning, teams are also empowered to take responsibility for their own learning. They are therefore provided with the mechanisms they need if they are to learn and improve on their own terms. With effective group processes, teams are able to harness the collective brainpower of talented professionals from multiple disciplines to solve problems ranging from the straightforward to the complex, creating opportunities to develop a shared vision and organizational alignment. To become an effective team, groups of individuals need common goals, an understanding of one another's roles, established procedures and norms, and teaming competencies that can be drawn upon to ensure effective ongoing collaboration. When teams are able to take responsibility for their own learning, they are able to apply the collective wisdom of diverse individuals from multiple functional, technical, and cultural backgrounds, enabling the organization to solve problems and continually adapt and improve in ways that would otherwise be impossible. Later in this chapter, we will discuss the role of the multi-level learning coach, a trained facilitator of individual and organizational learning who is responsible for helping teams at all levels learn and adapt in the service of achieving high-performance results.

See the Whole

P. Peter Senge (2006) tells us that systems thinking is the glue that binds all the essential components of the learning organization together: personal mastery, shared vision, team learning, and mental models. Without systems thinking, organizations will find it hard to learn from experience and transform themselves to achieve higher levels of performance. Systems thinking helps us deal with the underlying root causes of problems rather than treating the symptoms. It helps us to look for patterns of behavior in organizations—ways of solving problems—that often lead to recurrence of the same problems over and over. Many of us have seen what happens when managers use Band-Aids to overcome short-term challenges, only to find little long-term relief. We've seen the effects of departmental units that blame one another for persistent problems rather than collaborating to deal with the root causes, thus limiting the performance of the organization as a whole. Take, for example, a large financial services firm that wanted to improve the way its business units were charged for technology services. The business units complained bitterly about the way they were being billed for internal services like telephones and servers, demanding more transparency so that they could see what the charges were based on. The CIO implemented a new system for tracking these charges that was intended to enable the business units to view the drivers of their costs, like the number of telephones or printers that they used on an ongoing basis. The new system required the business units themselves to notify the technology group when employees changed locations or left the firm altogether. The business units, however, were not willing to spend the time required to provide this information, and the CIO refused to provide the resources to do so because he saw it as the business units' responsibility. The new system wound up not dealing with the root causes of the original problems. The business units continued to complain, and the organization continued to overspend and overbill for its technology resources. Systems thinking helps organizations see the overall effects of behavioral patterns like these that limit the performance of the organization as a whole.

Use a Third-Party Coach

Retrospectives at frequent intervals during the project's life cycle are the primary means for facilitating learning and continuous innovation in multi-level learning. Retrospectives, as discussed in the previous section, enable teams to systematically learn from experience so that they can improve upon their strategies, reduce the risk of failures and surprises, and deliver high-quality outputs for internal and external customers. As we shall see in the next chapter, engaging a multi-level learning coach from outside a team's immediate reporting structure is critical for promoting effective learning and reflection. The multi-level learning coach has no decision-making authority and serves in a substantively neutral role in this respect, helping teams reduce the damaging effects of defensive routines and helping team members at all levels overcome avoidance mechanisms that prevent the discussion of difficult, challenging, or threatening topics. The coach helps teams establish effective mechanisms for collaboration, and frees executives and managers to focus on refining their strategies and improving the way in which work gets done so that they can contribute their knowledge and expertise. The role of the multi-level learning coach will be discussed in more detail in the next section.

Reflect at Multiple Levels

Structured reflection is not limited to the project team. In multi-level learning, retrospectives are conducted after action at each of three critical levels: project, process, and strategy. In some organizations, these levels of learning may mirror responsibilities within the organizational hierarchy, yet their purpose is not to perpetuate unnecessary layers of management and bureaucracy or to restrict the type of learning at any level. Rather, the layers parallel Mezirow's levels of reflection. As discussed earlier in this chapter, these levels are content, process, and premise reflection. The first level, content reflection, is the type of reflection that is typical of a project team retrospective, where the team focuses on reviewing how ideas have been applied in solving problems at each stage of a project. The second level, process reflection, is also important for teams, yet it is the type of reflection that is typical of a project management office (PMO) or program manager, whose task is to help project managers improve the processes common to multiple projects. The third level, premise reflection, is typical of the type of reflection required at the senior management level, where the primary task is to ensure that the organization is solving the right problems to begin with, and that the right projects and programs have been selected to achieve the organization's strategy.

These layers do not imply that project teams cannot or should not utilize premise reflection, for example, or that senior managers need not engage in content reflection. Rather, the three levels of reflection are aimed at helping applicable organizational members reflect in the ways that are most productive for achieving their tasks. Shareholders do not hold project teams accountable for setting the right strategy. Likewise, senior managers need to empower project teams to deliver project work successfully. Reflecting at three levels promotes the type of reflection for each constituency that is the best fit with the task at hand. Its purpose is not to create or embed unnecessary hierarchy, but to facilitate productive reflection among the right people at the right time.

While focusing the right type of reflection at the right level is important, it is also valuable to enable members at each level to identify problems that affect their performance, even if these problems require deeper or higher levels of reflection. For example, if a project team finds that the senior management team is continually choosing the wrong projects, it is important that this feedback be provided in the right way at the right time.

CONCLUSION

Many of the foundations and principles of multi-level learning have been put to use by many organizations, including Intel, the U.S. Army, and a growing number of IT organizations that have adopted agile development approaches. The core of multi-level learning is the before- and after-action meetings: the prospective and the retrospective. These meetings, especially the retrospective, are facilitated by a skilled third-party coach who helps individuals and teams continually innovate, adapt, and improve their performance. Multi-level learning builds on agile and lean thinking and is founded on a number of principles, including satisfy the customer, eliminate waste, welcome new insights, empower team learning, see the whole, use a third-party coach, and reflect at multiple levels.

In the next chapter, we discuss the multi-level learning coach and his role in helping teams and individuals at all levels to continually improve performance.

PART 2

Roles

3 | THE MULTI-LEVEL LEARNING COACH

Organizations will require help in moving from traditional project and program management to an adaptive, continuous systems-level learning approach. The multi-level learning coach helps organizations make this journey by providing objective, substantively neutral facilitation and coaching that helps teams learn from experience, adapt to changing conditions, and continuously improve their performance. You may be interested in stepping into this role yourself, or you may want to find someone who can play this role for you or for your client's organization. Either way, this chapter begins with an overview of the role of the multi-level learning coach, then moves to a discussion of the importance of neutrality and objectivity, the skills required of those serving in this role, the core values of group facilitation, the basics of effective group process, and guidance on how the multi-level learning coach can intervene to help groups reflect, learn, and improve.

OVERVIEW OF THE MULTI-LEVEL LEARNING COACH ROLE

As an experienced hand, the multi-level learning coach works to build the organization's ongoing capability for continuous improvement at three levels: project, process, and strategy. She works with program managers, project managers, project management office (PMO) personnel, and senior leaders to devise practical ways to integrate action-reflection cycles into the organization's ongoing work routines. The multi-level learning coach often begins her work by introducing the senior management team to multi-level learning. She helps them develop a plan for weaving these practices into the way business gets done. She then works with senior managers to conduct a strategic prospective, helping them to clarify the organization's strategic vision and the roles and responsibilities of senior management team members in making the vision a reality. At the conclusion of the first iteration, stage, or phase, which lasts anywhere from one to three months, the coach facilitates a strategic retrospective, at which the senior team reflects on the actual results delivered and adjusts and improves its strategy, priorities, and project portfolio as a result.

At the process level, the multi-level learning coach works with the PMO, if one exists, to facilitate cross-project improvement. The coach conducts action-reflection cycles with project managers to improve processes that are common to multiple projects. PMOs are well positioned to bring innovations from one project team to the next once these improvements are identified. However, many PMOs aren't yet fully equipped to play this knowledge brokering role. Instead, despite the best of intentions, they focus on promulgating rules and enforcing standards, often with limited feedback from project managers and teams. They may neglect to involve others in action-reflection cycles aimed at improving the processes they define. In the next chapter, we address how PMOs can become more effective in this role.

At the project level, the multi-level learning coach teams up with the project manager or the agile scrum master to facilitate regular action-reflection cycles with project teams. The first of these cycles begins with a "prospective" that is conducted at project kickoff, where the team clarifies its long- and short-term objectives, its roles and responsibilities, and its operating norms, as well as its near-term tasks and deliverables. After approximately 30 days or upon completion of each iteration or phase, the coach conducts a retrospective, at which the team reviews what it intended to accomplish in that time period, what was actually delivered, the reasons for the results attained, and what can be done to sustain or improve those results for the next time period.

At Intel, skilled, neutral facilitators are responsible for preparing, conducting, and following up on project and program retrospectives (Lavell & Martinelli, 2008c). To prepare for these sessions, the facilitator works with senior managers to define the objectives, identify attendees, and gather preliminary data on a team's progress and results. The facilitator then conducts the meeting with the project team and subsequently assists in conducting a management "report-out" to share good practices with other projects and programs that might benefit from the improvements that result.

Initially, the coach may conduct all of the organization's retrospectives, including those at the strategy, process, and project levels. Yet to enable the organization to expand its multi-level learning capabilities, the coach works to develop the skills of other high-potential facilitators so that they can begin conducting these sessions on their own. These trained facilitators then move toward becoming coaches themselves, helping others adopt the skills necessary to help the organization learn, adapt, and continually innovate from one project to the next. By the end of 2008, Intel had 65 trained facilitators who were capable of conducting retrospectives (Lavell & Martinelli, 2008a).

THE IMPORTANCE OF NEUTRALITY AND OBJECTIVITY

It is important that multi-level-learning coaches and facilitators come from outside a given team's immediate organizational reporting structure and that they do not have an investment in any agenda other than facilitating learning and continuous improvement. This means, for example, that the facilitator for strategic retrospectives should not report to the senior management team. Likewise, it also means that the facilitator or coach should not be responsible for managing the individual performance of project team members, nor should he use information obtained as part of his work to influence individual performance reviews or personnel decisions. Although this may raise the eyebrows of managers at first, it is an important principle of multi-level learning. As discussed earlier in this chapter, learning is enhanced by objective, skilled facilitation that helps teams overcome communication barriers and defensive routines, both of which can be exacerbated if the discussion leader is perceived as favoring certain people, viewpoints, strategies, or approaches over others. Facilitation by someone other than an objective, unbiased third party can keep important issues buried, leading to continued frustration, avoidance patterns, and less than optimal performance.

Ronald Cervero and Arthur Wilson (2001) assert that learning in any context represents a struggle for knowledge and power. Not only is learning shaped by power relations, but it plays a role in reproducing or changing these relations. Taking this perspective, the negotiation of meaning associated with reflecting on project and program experiences can also be seen as a political endeavor. This means that it is important that the facilitator or coach not be a representative of one of the potentially competing interests at the table. When the facilitator has a specific agenda other than enhancing learning, his underlying assumptions—whether explicit or implicit, hidden or overt—can distort and bias learning and reflection in that direction, whether intentionally or not. While there is no such thing as a truly "neutral" facilitator, having a skilled, objective facilitator whose agenda is to help teams learn and improve helps to overcome the damaging effects of defensiveness, bias, blame, and avoidance, all of which are symptoms of deeper issues that need to be addressed if a team's talents are to be best utilized to achieve its objectives.

SKILLS REQUIRED OF THE MULTI-LEVEL LEARNING COACH

The multi-level learning coach needs to have skills and knowledge in at least four specific areas. She needs to be a highly effective group facilitator, to be able to ask questions that generate deep insight, to help members navigate organizational change, and to be familiar with the business and technical context within which the team members conduct their work. A discussion of each of these areas follows.

First and foremost, the coach needs many of the skills required of effective group facilitators. These include the ability to listen, observe, and remember behaviors and conversation; to communicate clearly; to understand the differences and similarities among various perspectives; to analyze and synthesize topics of conversation; to elicit and identify underlying assumptions; to diagnose and intervene to improve group effectiveness; to provide feedback without creating defensive routines; to accept feedback without reacting defensively; to monitor and reflect on one's own behavior; to develop trust; to empathize with others; to provide support and encouragement; and to have patience (Schwarz, 2002).

Second, in addition to these basic facilitation skills, the multi-level learning coach must also have the ability to foster productive reflection so that the organization can learn from its experiences in ways that would not be possible without such intervention. The coach must therefore have the ability to ask the right questions at the right time—questions that foster reflection to help clarify goals and roles, as is often the case in prospectives, or questions that enable teams to learn from their recent experience, as is the case in retrospectives. In this regard, the multi-level learning coach mirrors the role that an action learning coach might play in the context of an action learning project. In action learning, teams are assembled with the explicit aim of developing the professional talents and skills of employees or managers by providing frequent opportunities for reflection in a structured format (O'Neil & Marsick, 2007). Team members may work on problems that pertain to their individual circumstances, using the group to aid their understanding of both the problem and the range of solutions, or they may work collectively on a single organizational challenge, asking questions that focus reflection on a single problem that is critical to the organization. In both cases, an action learning coach may assist the group by asking—and helping others ask—"discriminating questions" or "fresh questions" that foster deeper insights. Judy O'Neil and Victoria Marsick (2007) provide a number of examples of questions that may be used to help teams understand what's happening or not happening with their project, determine what should happen next, build on previous progress, stay on track, transfer recent learning to their day-to-day job, or provide feedback to teammates.

The third family of skills required of the multi-level learning coach involves helping members navigate organizational change. Because the coach also serves as a catalyst for introducing reflective practices into organizational routines, he must also be cognizant of the larger cultural and political forces that affect the organization, its people, and the communities of practice within which they work. It is naïve to think that the multi-level learning coach can remain aloof from these factors. Attempting to do so may lead to interventions that damage relationships or undermine the effectiveness of structured learning. Instead, the coach helps people to navigate difficult terrain in a way that ensures their long-term commitment to learning and improvement. Through discussions with both individuals and groups, the multi-level learning coach helps people identify key stakeholders, understand their positions and points of view, and identify the underlying needs that drive their actions, behaviors, and decisions. In this way, he better assists the organization in improving its ability to learn and adapt, helping people work collaboratively to more effectively overcome the defensive routines and dysfunctions that block improvement and innovation.

Debra Lavell and Russ Martinelli (2008b) learned a number of lessons about organizational change as they championed the introduction of retrospectives into the product development process at Intel. First, they suggest that coaches should start with a problem, not a solution. This means that coaches first need to understand and clarify their internal client's problem, then find ways retrospectives can help solve those problems, not the other way around. Second, they found it important to start small and establish "pull" once demonstrable results were achieved, rather than to attempt large-scale deployment right away. That meant that at Intel, the coach began by working with a manager who she thought would be open to the idea and subsequently gained approval to hold a two-hour face-to-face meeting with a small team to pilot the approach. The overwhelmingly positive feedback led to the manager's championing the approach in other business units across Intel. By the end of the first year, the coach had conducted 15 retrospectives in that business unit alone.

Lavell and Martinelli also learned that it was important to tailor the methodology as needed to expand upon its effectiveness and adapt it to the organization's specific culture and needs. They found, for example, that holding retrospectives at three key times during a project or program's life cycle was more effective than just conducting a postproject review. This enabled project teams to capture learnings as they occurred, while the memories were still fresh in their minds, so that they could capture benefits while the projects were "in flight" rather than at the end.

The coaches at Intel found that while it was critical to start small, the momentum for retrospectives "bubbled up" to the senior management level many times. As senior managers began to see the benefits of these retrospectives, they provided additional support, and this led to a broader number of teams adopting the approach, including even those that had previously stayed away from such practices.

The fourth and final skill area required of successful multi-level learning coaches is a familiarity with the specific project environment, the nature of the business, and the content of the work upon which they are helping teams reflect. When the coach does not have sufficient knowledge of the work environment, whether it be software development, product development, research and development, process and operations improvement, engineering, or construction, she risks not being able to understand what's being communicated and may not be able to intervene effectively. This can undermine both the credibility of the coaching and the practice of productive reflection.

Most teams understand that a facilitator of learning is not an expert in the work that is being performed. However, if the group members feel that they are not being understood, or that they are spending too much time "educating" the facilitator, the learning process will be severely undermined, and group members will be left with the feeling that they have been wasting their time. Under no circumstances is this a desirable way for them to feel. Therefore, it is important that the coach not be a pure "facilitator," but that she also know many of the ins and outs of the language, work environment, business processes, and strategies of the business or group she is helping improve. This is accomplished either through having experience in the specific work environment or through conversations with key "informants" who can help her to better understand the organizational context and culture.

Clearly, the skills required of the multi-level learning coach take time to develop. Yet the coach's capabilities in the areas of group facilitation, questioning insight, organizational change, and knowledge of the business are vital components in making multi-level learning part of the fabric of the organization. We now turn to a review of some of the basics of group effectiveness and how coaches can help groups learn, reflect, and continuously improve.

THREE CORE VALUES FOR EFFECTIVE FACILITATION

Roger Schwarz (1994), adapting the work of Chris Argyris and Donald Schön, defines three core values of effective group intervention: valid information, free and informed choice, and internal commitment. These values underpin the role of the multi-level learning coach and represent a worldview concerning what it takes to facilitate effective group interactions. The first value, valid information, means that all information that is relevant to a point of view is shared so that others can independently determine whether that information is true. It also means that people understand what is being communicated. The second value, free and informed choice, means that people are able to make decisions that are based on valid information. It also means that people are not coerced or manipulated into acting or behaving in a certain way. Facilitators, therefore, are not given the task of "changing behavior." Rather, they provide information that enables others to decide whether or not they wish to change their behavior. If they choose to do so, the facilitator helps them with a path forward. The third value, internal commitment to the choice, means that people feel personally responsible for the choices they make, and that these choices are "intrinsically compelling or satisfying" (Schwarz, 1994, p. 8).

The multi-level learning coach may find these values to be very useful in their work with teams, and would be well served by modeling these values as they intervene. That's because, as discussed in Chapter 2, defensive routines are so prevalent in organizational contexts, particularly under conditions of red-light learning, that they actively work against enabling people to make free and informed choices. When reacting defensively, "saving face," or avoiding embarrassment or threat, people may omit, avoid, or even distort information that would enable others to fully understand a given problem, its causes, and its antecedents. This means that the root causes of problems may remain unresolved and performance may continue to suffer, much to the chagrin of everyone involved. More often than not, when people are less able to make free and informed choices, they don't bring their best to their work. Instead, they may merely comply with short-term dictates rather than finding creative ways to apply their unique talents and skills to solve most pressing challenges.

Ideally, the core values of facilitation create a self-reinforcing cycle, as shown in Figure 3.1. Team members in effective groups will require valid information in order to make free and informed choices about how to implement strategies, improve processes, and overcome obstacles. When they are able to make free and informed choices, they are more likely to become internally committed to making the resulting improvements. Once the changes are implemented, team members will seek out valid information about the effectiveness of these changes so that they

FIGURE 3.1
The Three Core Values of Effective Intervention

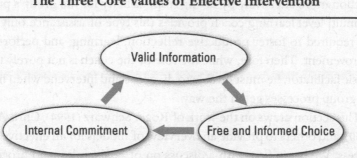

can make free and informed choices about any adjustments that need to be made.

It is important to note that while these values form the basis of the role of the multi-level learning coach, the values themselves mean that the members need to choose whether these values work for them in a free and informed way. The coach needs to be clear that these are the values she brings to her work and that members have the choice to adopt them as they see fit. The role of the coach is not to "enforce" these values, but to provide them as a set of ideals that can be modeled effectively, providing clarity not only on what can make for effective facilitation, but also on what makes for effective group interaction.

MODELS FOR EFFECTIVE GROUP PROCESS

Group process is how a group works together, including how its members communicate, solve problems, make decisions, handle conflict, and manage the boundaries between themselves and the larger organization (Schein, 1999; Schwarz, 2002). Group process can be contrasted conceptually with a group's content, which is the work that a team has set out to achieve and is represented in strategic plans, process maps, procedures, and project plans. The multi-level learning coach is best served by using an appropriate model of effective group functioning so that he can intervene to help teams collaborate more effectively when they get off track, or when certain behaviors, actions, or routines block the ability of people to learn together. While the role of a basic facilitator is to help a group function more effectively by taking responsibility for the group's process, the multi-level learning coach provides this type of assistance only when it is required to foster productive reflection, learning, and performance improvement. Therefore, while the role of the coach is not purely that of a basic facilitator, he must be able to diagnose and intervene when ineffective group processes get in the way.

This section draws on the work of Roger Schwarz (1994), Chris Argyris (1990), and others to provide an overview of models for an effective group process. We begin first with a discussion of goals, roles, and procedures and their importance for effective teams. We then move to an overview of models for effective group processes, including communication, problem solving, decision making, and boundary management. We then conclude this chapter with guidance on how the multi-level learning coach might use these models to diagnose and intervene with groups in order to improve the groups' processes and enhance their learning capacity.

GOALS, ROLES, AND PROCEDURES

When people get together to accomplish a task, especially if they come from a variety of communities of practice, backgrounds, or functional disciplines, their capacity and effectiveness as a group depend in large part upon the level of clarity in their goals, roles, and procedures for working together (Berlew, 1993; Rubin et al., 1975). The pyramid in Figure 3.2 depicts these elements in a hierarchical fashion in a way that can be useful for facilitators. Each component depends on the one above it. For example, it is important to be clear about the task or goal to be accomplished before selecting people to fill specific roles. At the top of the pyramid, therefore, are a group's goals. Most of us who have been members of teams have firsthand knowledge of how important it is to have clear goals that everyone accepts, whether the team is an athletic team, a unit in the armed services, a senior management group, or a project team. It is for this reason that preaching the importance of having clear, accepted goals may not be nearly as helpful as actually making it happen. Questions for groups include: Do all members of the group share the same vision of what they are trying to accomplish or create? Are the goals clear and unambiguous?

FIGURE 3.2
Goals, Roles, and Procedures

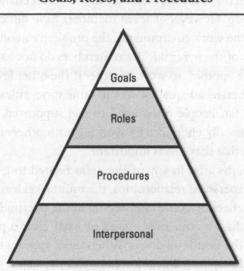

Goals

Roles

Procedures

Interpersonal

Are there conflicting goals among group members that might impede the accomplishment of the collective aim? Does each team member agree with the goals, or should they be modified or enhanced to ensure that everyone can live with them?

Roles are the next component in the sequence; they can be addressed after taking a pass at goal clarification. Clear, conflict-free roles are the ideal. Questions for groups include: Is everyone familiar with the skills, capabilities, and talents that each person brings to the effort? Do team members know what to expect from one another? Are there any concerns about whether everyone can carry out her role, and if so, what can be done to resolve this potential conflict? In practice, it is not always possible to have an ideal level of clarity on goals and roles, yet running through these questions can help a team get started and prevent surprises or disappointments later on.

The next level down in the pyramid is procedures. Without basic working procedures that are agreed upon at some level, it will be difficult for a group, especially one with new members, to accomplish its work in a productive way. Procedures, also referred to as group processes, include communication, problem solving, decision making, and boundary management, each of which is discussed later in this section.

At the bottom of the pyramid are interpersonal relationships. If people like to work with one another, then they have a better chance of becoming an effective group. However, if team members have difficulty relating to one another in the work environment, the problem can often be traced to the upper levels of the pyramid. Team members do not have to be friends (or even like one another) to work together if the other levels in the pyramid can be addressed adequately. At the same time, rules and structures can go only so far. People often need to feel supported, included, and, hopefully, intrinsically energized by working with others in the group on a collective task that they feel is important.

When problems arise in any of the areas related to goals, roles, procedures, or interpersonal relationships, the multi-level learning coach can help the team reflect by going one step up in the pyramid to ensure clarity at that level first, as this may in and of itself clear a path for solving the problem at the next level down. When there appears to be confusion about roles and responsibilities, for example, the coach might help the team go one level up in the pyramid to ensure that its goals are clear. Doing so may lead to a more productive discussion about roles and responsibilities. It may take more than one iteration, of course, for goals, roles, and procedures to be clarified, yet this can be a very useful tool for multi-level learning coaches, particularly in conducting prospective sessions (or before-action reviews) prior to executing a strategy, implementing a process improvement, or planning the next stage, phase, or iteration of a project or program.

We now turn to a more in-depth discussion of models for effective group procedures, more commonly called group processes.

Communication

Our ability to communicate with others is the foundation for all other group processes. It underlies everything we do. As such, ineffective communication can be a powerful inhibitor of group effectiveness and collective learning, particularly within the context of the strains of organizational life (Argyris, 1990). Chris Argyris and Donald Schön have done extensive research on how people undermine both their own effectiveness and that of their organization by enacting defensive routines that block learning and create "self-sealing" perspectives that freeze organizations in place, restricting improvement and the achievement of important goals. In Chapter 1, we discussed how defensive routines, often triggered by red-light learning, can lead to blame, bias, distortions, and the inability of project and program teams to resolve problems effectively in sustainable ways. Multi-level learning works to build reflection and learning into work routines on a continuous, systematic basis so that people are not thrust into these situations only when problems occur. Yet potential embarrassment, face-saving, and the perception of personal threat often lie just under the surface, even when everything appears to be working fine. The multi-level learning coach, in his objective, substantively neutral role, can help groups at all levels mitigate the effects of defensive routines by diagnosing and intervening to facilitate more effective communication patterns. This can enable groups to resolve problems proactively before they snowball into larger issues, blowups, and surprises that trigger a red light on the status report.

The Ladder of Inference (Argyris, 1990) is a model that can help us better understand how our perceptions create a self-reinforcing loop in which our individual beliefs influence what information we select and hear, and how what we select and hear influences the actions that we subsequently take. As people react to one another's behavior, the Ladder of Inference works unconsciously in the background and can explain how information that goes untested and unvalidated in our own heads can undermine our ability to communicate effectively, leading to escalations in conflict and organizational dysfunction.

We will use as an example an interaction between two people that occurred on a large-scale global project that was ultimately cancelled. The goal of the project was to select and implement an enterprisewide software package, one that would eventually affect thousands of employees. The CIO of the company considered it a mission-critical project. A conflict arose between two managers on the team. The first was Bernard, who was assigned the responsibility for "developing the high-level strategy." The second was Tracy, who was responsible for translating this strategy into "detailed requirements." Neither manager had done this type of project before, and both had expressed concerns about whether or not the project would succeed.

Bernard, having finished the high-level strategy document, said to Tracy, "I've completed my part of the project plan, which was to develop a high-level strategy. It's now your responsibility to translate the strategy into detailed requirements." In reaction, Tracy responded, "This is not useful to me; it's too high-level. You need to take another crack at it." Bernard, in response, said, "Of course it's high-level. That's the point of it. It's high-level requirements. That was my part of the project plan. Now you need to take this to the next level so that the team can select the right software." The interaction continued in this way for a while, ultimately leading to a stalemate. Unfortunately, the managers worked in different locations, one in London, and one in New York. After they left the meeting, they did not see each other again for quite some time, and the problem remained unresolved for days, then weeks.

In the background, both Tracy and Bernard may have been climbing the Ladder of Inference during this interaction. As shown in Figure 3.3, at the bottom of the ladder are observable data—statements, behaviors, and gestures that can be readily observed, as on a video recorder. Observing these statements, Tracy and Bernard may have selected certain data based on their personal filters, and ascribed meaning to these statements based on their previous experience. They then may have moved rapidly up the ladder, making assumptions about each other, drawing conclusions that ultimately led to another observable response, and so on. The tricky part, however, is that much of this happens in the background—in people's heads—and is based on each individual's assumptions and beliefs, which are shaped by that person's individual experiences. Tracy, for example, may have selected the data "it's your responsibility." She may then have taken this to mean that she was the one who would be blamed if it wasn't done right. Climbing up the ladder of inference, she may have assumed (or feared) that she didn't have the knowledge and/or skills to take the next step, and that Bernard was attempting to skirt the responsibility himself for the same reasons. Her conclusion might have been, "He's setting me up to avoid getting blamed himself." She may have acted on this belief by attempting to place the responsibility back on Bernard by explaining to him that he needed to improve the document before she could work with it.

It may be that both managers were engaging in defensive routines as they climbed the Ladder of Inference. Although we will never know what each of these managers was actually thinking, it's possible that each was

FIGURE 3.3
The Ladder of Inference [Adapted from Argyris (1990)]

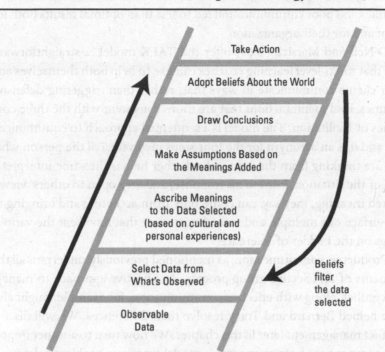

Take Action

Adopt Beliefs About the World

Draw Conclusions

Make Assumptions Based on the Meanings Added

Ascribe Meanings to the Data Selected (based on cultural and personal experiences)

Select Data from What's Observed

Observable Data

Beliefs filter the data selected

trying to avoid embarrassment or threat by placing demands on the other. As touched upon in Chapter 1, Argyris (1995) describes organizational defensive routines as "any action, policy, or practice that prevents organizational participants from experiencing embarrassment or threat and, at the same time, prevents them from discovering the causes of the embarrassment or threat" (pp. 20–22). Perhaps both managers thought that they did not have the skills required to enable the project to succeed, and because of their escalating conflict, they may have become even more invested in "winning" by placing responsibility on the other party in order to avoid personal failure.

Because climbing the Ladder of Inference occurs in the minds of other people, it's impossible to know what Bernard and Tracy were thinking at the time. However, what is known is that the project was delayed for weeks because of this stalemate, and that this ultimately led to the project's being cancelled by the CIO. Both managers were reassigned to roles with significantly less responsibility, which leads us to believe that their defensive routines and poor communication led to less than optimal results both for them and for their organization.

O'Neil and Marsick (2007) offer the TALK model, a straightforward tool that multi-level learning coaches can use to help both themselves and their clients communicate in ways that, rather than triggering defensive routines, lead to interactions that are more consistent with the three core values of facilitation. The model is a sequential approach to communicating, and it is an acronym for the four steps involved: *Tell* the person what you are thinking from the start, *ask* whether he has the same interpretation of the situation, *listen* to his response, and *keep* open to others' views. Shared meaning, they say, can come only from accepting and bringing to the surface our multiple understandings, those that represent the various rungs on the Ladder of Inference.

Productive communication, as mentioned previously, underpins all the elements of an effective group process. An effective approach to managing conflict, along with effective communication, for example, might also have helped Bernard and Tracy resolve their differences. We will discuss conflict management later in this chapter. We now turn to another important component of group process, a model for group problem solving.

Problem Solving

Much of a team's work is focused on problems. Problems in this context are simply a gap between what is desired and what currently exists. The central elements of problem solving are the following steps, which can be seen both on a macro level (in project plans, for example) or on a micro level (in meeting agendas focused on more specific issues): Identify the problem, collect data about the problem, analyze the data to determine the root causes, develop possible solutions, select the most appropriate solution, implement the solution, and evaluate and monitor the situation after implementation. Project methodologies such as Six Sigma, TQM, and other quality improvement approaches build these steps directly into project plans in order to generate sustainable improvements that focus not just on symptoms, but on solving the root causes of problems so that they don't recur.

Most readers will find nothing conceptually difficult about this model and may even be wondering why such a basic topic is being addressed here. The hard part about working with groups is not helping them understand the model, it's helping individuals clarify what stage of the problem-solving process they are in so that they can collaborate effectively at each stage. This becomes the basis for the multi-level learning coach to intervene to help people focus on the right place at the right time. This is consistent with the value described earlier of helping teams acquire valid information that enables individuals to make free and informed choices.

Decision Making

Groups use a variety of ways to make decisions, some more formal than others, and some more important than others in their scope and magnitude. Yet effective decision making is essential if people are to work together productively in a team format. Decision making includes who should be involved, when, in what decisions, and how the choice will be made (Schwarz, 1994). An effective decision has the following characteristics: It takes all relevant data into account, team members accept it and will work to implement it, and the decision is made in an appropriate amount of time. Again, these characteristics are consistent with the ideals of valid information, free and informed choice, and internal commitment. While not all decisions need to be made by consensus, these three ideals point to the superiority of consensus for helping people make free and informed choices to which they are internally committed. However, time and resource limitations don't always enable full consensus to be achieved, and not all decisions require such investment. The coach, team leader, and group members should decide in advance the who, when, what, and how of decision making before significant choices that affect group members and stakeholders in the organization have to be made.

A useful model for clarifying decision processes entails identifying who should *recommend* the appropriate course of action, who should *approve* the decision, who should be *consulted* prior to the decision's being made, and who should be *informed* after the fact. This model, called the RACI model, helps clarify the roles of individuals inside and outside the team in the decision-making process. In situations in which consensus is desirable and the time can be dedicated to achieving it, all group members would be assigned *A*, for approve. Often, however, a subgroup or an individual with expertise in a specific area may recommend a course of action to the entire group. In such cases, this person or subgroup would be labeled *R*. In still other cases, people may not want to either recommend or approve a decision, but instead should be consulted beforehand so their opinion can be considered. Finally, those assigned an *I* would not have influence over the decision but would be notified of the result in an appropriate amount of time.

The coach can help teams establish effective decision making not only in team meetings, but for the project organization overall. For example, many project groups have established "gates" through which projects must pass, such as before systems "go live" or prior to the implementation of recommendations on a process improvement project. Often, these decision points are critical not only for project teams, but for stakeholders in many parts of the organization. Clarification on who should be involved, when, and how can help project organizations improve the way they manage these important milestones.

Conflict Resolution

The Chinese *kanji* characters for "conflict" represent both "danger" and "opportunity." While conflict can sometimes be threatening, it also opens up avenues for collaboration that would not otherwise be possible. Conflict is a natural aspect of group activity that, when handled effectively, can promote creative solutions by combining the interests, skills, and capabilities of diverse people and perspectives. From this point of view, conflict at some level may even be necessary if organizations are to surmount substantive obstacles and deal with their most important challenges. Conflict is defined here simply as a situation in which two or more parties have interests or needs that differ in some way and that need to be resolved in order for a group to move forward. Interests and needs can be either tangible or psychological. And they must be satisfied in some way (or changed) for the individuals involved to reach a sustainable outcome. Examples of tangible needs include equipment, tools, and resources to perform a task. Psychological needs include things like respect, autonomy, recognition, belonging, and safety.

A useful framework for understanding the differences in how people relate to conflict—and a path forward for helping teams become more effective at handling it—is reflected in the dual concerns model depicted in Figure 3.4, a version of which is incorporated into the Thomas-Kilmann conflict mode instrument (Kilmann & Thomas, 1977). The horizontal axis represents the degree to which an individual or group is attempting to satisfy others' concerns. The vertical axis represents the degree to which someone is attempting to satisfy her own concerns. The result leads to five different styles that people bring to conflict situations: competing, avoiding, accommodating, compromising, and collaborating. The approach that is most suitable for a given situation depends on the degree to which an ongoing relationship needs to be maintained and the importance of the outcome to participants. For example, if an individual inadvertently says something that is irritating or offensive to another, it may be worth avoiding, given the low degree of severity and impact. However, in situations where two or more individuals are responsible for making choices that affect others in a significant way, such as in the case of important project decisions, strategy formulation, or process designs, a collaborative approach to negotiating a successful outcome is preferable, as it enables multiple perspectives to be combined. No party to the decision "caves in," tries to "win" at the expense of others, avoids the decision, or compromises his views to accommodate others. Rather, each fully represents her point of view, advocating it with an appropriate level of assertiveness and with an appropriate degree of cooperation that seeks to inquire and understand the underlying basis for others' points of view.

In their book *Getting to Yes*, Roger Fisher and William Ury (1991) outline a number of steps that participants can take to resolve conflicts in a collaborative way, reaching outcomes that satisfy all parties' needs in a win-win fashion. They help us to realize that bargaining over positions can often lead to ineffective solutions, with results that are potentially damaging to the people involved. Positions can be viewed as opening demands, and may come in the form of something like, "We don't have additional resources to put into this effort." They can come in the form of posturing or blaming as a way of protecting one's own interests, as when someone says, "You've consumed enough time from our department on this project already."

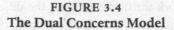

FIGURE 3.4
The Dual Concerns Model

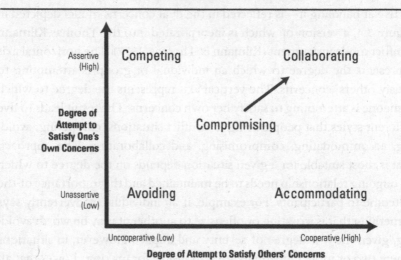

For a multi-level learning coach, it is important to help people move beyond these initial positions to identify, understand, and satisfy the underlying needs that give rise to them. When the underlying needs are understood, and each party agrees on what those needs are, it is possible to reframe the problem from the initial positions to find a solution that meets each party's underlying needs. The IT department's position might be that it needs more people from the call center to test its new software application, while the call center manager's position might be that she can't provide more people because their time needs to be dedicated to serving customers. Reframing helps people move beyond these initial positions to meet the underlying needs that generated them in the first place. The problem can then become, "How can we satisfy the IT group's need to ensure that the new software application for the call center is free of 'bugs' and, at the same time, enable the call center to maintain the high levels of service that customers expect while the software is being tested?" This can lead to more creative solutions than those available by bargaining over the initial positions. For example, the two groups might agree to move up the software implementation so that it does not coincide with a peak time for customer service, enabling IT to get the people it needs for testing while enabling the call center to meet its service-level goals at the same time.

The multi-level learning coach can intervene by helping people focus on how their behaviors might create a win-lose situation, or one in which someone caves in for fear of asserting her needs. Ellen Raider, Susan Coleman, and Janet Gerson (Raider et al., 2006) offer a simple yet useful mnemonic tool, AEIOU, that helps to distinguish between productive and nonproductive behaviors in conflict situations. Each letter signifies the first letter of a type of behavior that is typical in these situations. Starting with the first, *attacking* behaviors include threats, hostile words or gestures, insults, defending, criticizing, interrupting, and asking judgmental questions, to name a few. These often lead to escalation of the conflict rather than resolution. *Evading* behaviors are also unproductive, and include changing the subject, withdrawing, postponing, or not acknowledging the issues to begin with. *Informing* behaviors can be useful, because they enable people to state their needs and justify their positions with facts. Informing behaviors should be used to help others understand the information being conveyed, enabling valid information to be shared and mutually understood. The next two types of behaviors—*opening* and *uniting* behaviors—are highly productive and generally lead to successful collaboration. Opening behaviors enable people to uncover the underlying needs of others. These include asking nonjudgmental questions about the other's position, needs, or feelings; actively listening by paraphrasing what was heard; and testing understanding and summarizing without necessarily agreeing. Uniting behaviors are also important because they not only bring people and perspectives together to set a tone that enables the sharing of underlying needs in a way that's suitable for all involved, but also enable joint solutions to be developed and relationships to continue in collaborative ways after resolution of the conflict. Uniting behaviors include ritual sharing to build rapport, establishing common ground, and reframing a problem to develop solutions that meet both sides' needs.

By keeping this simple mnemonic in mind, the multi-level learning coach can intervene with teams to help them distinguish collaborative behaviors from those that more often than not lead to avoidance, blame, or defensiveness and therefore leave problems unresolved, creating the opportunity for continuing frustration and poor performance.

We now turn to the fifth and final component of group process to be discussed, boundary management.

Boundary Management

Groups, whether they be senior management teams, departments, or project teams, are both differentiated from and integrated within a larger social structure consisting of many "communities of practice." As discussed in Appendix B, Etienne Wenger, Richard McDermott, and William Snyder (2002) define communities of practice as "groups of people who share a concern, a set of problems, or a passion about a topic, and who deepen their knowledge and expertise in this area by interacting on an ongoing basis" (p. 4). Just as groups of disparate people can develop into teams, so can teams develop into their own "communities of practice." Over time, through mutual engagement and joint enterprise, teams can develop a shared history that includes both tacit and explicit knowledge in the form of memories and a common repertoire of tools, methods, artifacts, and language. While communities of practice are highly effective at learning and continuously improving, through their work they also differentiate themselves from the larger organization. And it is this differentiation that creates the need to manage "practice boundaries" effectively, whether these boundaries lie between management teams and project groups or between functional groups like IT and marketing. Boundaries are a natural consequence of learning in communities of practice.

To manage boundaries effectively, especially for cross-functional teams that consist of members from multiple communities of practice, team members and project managers may be required to play a brokering role. Project managers leading cross-functional projects, for example, may belong to both a community of project management professionals associated with a PMO and a community of engineers within which their career has progressed. Brokering is the process of establishing connections between communities by "introducing elements of one practice into another" through processes of translation, coordination, and alignment between perspectives (Wenger, 1998, p. 105). Translation involves the rendering of something written or spoken in one community's words into the language and practices used in another. Coordination involves facilitating connections and transactions between communities and their members. Alignment involves addressing and resolving conflicting interests among two or more communities of practice.

Wenger elaborates further on the role and competencies required of brokers:

It requires enough legitimacy to influence the development of a practice, mobilize attention, and address conflicting interests. It also requires the ability to link practices by facilitating transactions between them, and to cause learning by introducing into a practice elements of another. (Wenger, 1998, p. 109)

Multi-level learning coaches can help members become effective brokers not only by helping them understand the nature of communities of practice as described in Appendix B, but also by reinforcing the tools of effective communication and conflict resolution described earlier in this chapter. Effective communication tools such as the Ladder of Inference and the TALK model can help people with different perspectives share their tacit knowledge—the knowledge that exists in their heads in the form of meanings, inferences, assumptions, and conclusions—which is difficult to uncover, particularly for those with different shared histories who come from different backgrounds. In addition, where conflicting interests appear to be at work, conflict resolution and effective collaboration are more probable when people seek to identify the underlying needs, reframe problems to address these needs, and find joint solutions that work for each party involved.

Multi-level learning coaches can not only help teams develop their own community of practice, but also encourage team members to seek solutions that include perspectives from multiple communities of practice, leading to more sustainable results and higher levels of collaboration.

Having discussed models for effective group processes, including communication, problem solving, decision making, conflict resolution, and boundary management, we now turn to a model for diagnosis and intervention that can guide multi-level learning coaches in their efforts to help groups learn and reflect in ways that are consistent with these models.

DIAGNOSING AND INTERVENING

Schwarz (2002) provides guidance for how to diagnose and intervene with groups to improve their effectiveness. The diagnosis-intervention cycle shown in Figure 3.5 is useful for multi-level learning coaches, as their role is to help teams develop both a climate and a group process that are conducive to productive learning and reflection. When the climate and conditions are perceived to be getting in the way, the multi-level learning coach may decide to intervene and help the team decide whether and how to change its patterns and actions so that it can move forward in a way that is more consistent with the models of effective group processes. The diagnosis-intervention cycle is important because it helps the coach herself remain consistent with the core values of facilitation, modeling the behavior for others as she intervenes.

The first three steps of the cycle occur in the mind of the facilitator and include (1) observing the behavior, (2) inferring meaning, and (3) deciding whether or not to intervene. These represent all the steps in the Ladder of Inference from observing behavior to drawing conclusions based on one's beliefs. Because these steps occur in the intervener's mind and are hidden from view, they must be communicated and tested with group members in order to remain consistent with the first core value of effective intervention: valid information. Therefore, the next two steps in the cycle are to (4) describe the observed behavior and (5) test the inferences with the others involved. In the final step, assuming that the group agrees with the facilitator's observations and inferences, she helps the group decide whether or not it wants to change its behavior and, if so, what course of action is most appropriate. The final steps are consistent with the last two core values of effective intervention: free and informed choice and internal commitment.

New facilitators may find this cycle threatening at first, because it invites open disagreement between the facilitator and the group members. Many corporate cultures, especially at managerial levels, do not reward discussion leaders for inviting disagreement, as this is perceived as possibly undermining the leader's credibility. For example, upon being encouraged to learn more about another department's goals and intentions, one senior manager with whom the author worked was quoted as saying, "I don't want to ask any questions to which I don't already know the

FIGURE 3.5
The Diagnosis-Intervention Cycle (Schwarz, 2002)

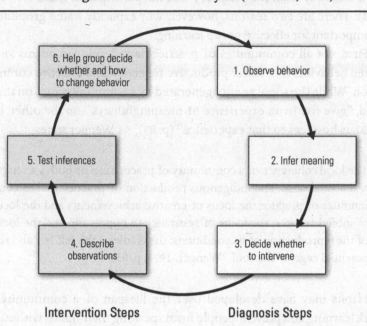

6. Help group decide whether and how to change behavior

1. Observe behavior

5. Test inferences

2. Infer meaning

4. Describe observations

3. Decide whether to intervene

Intervention Steps   **Diagnosis Steps**

answers." This is representative of the barriers some may face when making the transition to the role of coach or facilitator using the core values of facilitation. However, if the facilitator models these values successfully, team members will be provided with the information they need in order to decide whether and how to improve. If they decide to change, their internal commitment to doing so will lead to substantive improvements in the group's functioning and the potential for breakthroughs. As mentioned at the beginning of this chapter, the multi-level learning coach does not change behavior. He helps others decide whether or not they want to change, and if they do, supports them and encourages the formulation of a path forward.

GROUND RULES FOR GROUPS

When groups develop into effective teams, and when teams evolve their own community of practice, implicit ground rules become a matter of course.

New members of the group often have to learn these implicit rules as they work their way from the periphery into full participation (Lave & Wenger, 1991). There are two reasons, however, why explicitly stated ground rules are important for effective group learning.

First, not all communities of practice have developed norms and expected behaviors that foster productive reflection and effective communication. While the social energy generated by a community can, on the one hand, "give rise to an experience of meaningfulness," on the other, it can "hold us hostages to that experience" (p. 85). As Wenger states:

> The local coherence of a community of practice can be both a strength and a weakness. The indigenous production of practice makes communities of practice the locus of creative achievements and the locus of inbred failures; the locus of resistance to oppression and the locus of the reproduction of its conditions; the cradle of the self but also the potential cage of the soul. (Wenger, 1998, p. 85)

Habits may have developed over the lifespan of a community that block learning and prevent people from speaking their minds without fear of retribution. Some cultures or groups may shun the idea of reflection and learning, ascribing these processes to those who "don't know what they're doing"; this often is the result of ingrained defensive routines that have evolved to keep things just the way they are, whether they serve the organization, its stakeholders, and its employees or not. Having explicitly agreed-upon ground rules that help team members interact in more productive ways can create the space for new, more functional routines to develop that lead to improvements not only in strategies, programs, and projects, but also in how people feel about their work.

The second reason that ground rules are important stems from the nature of project work. In project environments, people are continually rotating into and out of various team roles. New teams are constantly being formed, and people must work with "new faces" who come from different cultures, business units, and functional backgrounds from both inside and outside their company, including strategic partners, newly acquired entities, vendors, suppliers, and customers. The demands placed on these teams require the delivery of quick results before a team is able to develop into a community of practice. While project charters and project plans explicitly define objectives and the roles of the individuals involved, they do not provide direction for how people might interact during group sessions. And teams from such diverse communities that need to deliver quickly cannot afford to leave group norms to chance, especially because each individual will have different interpretations of what constitutes effectiveness. Explicitly agreed-upon behavioral norms can prevent frustration among even the most gifted and talented people.

Each group should develop ground rules that enable each individual to feel a sense of safety when negotiating goals and roles or when reflecting on recent results. In difficult situations, particularly where individuals may not be accustomed to retrospectives or where a failure has recently occurred, Norm Kerth (2001) suggests that facilitators conduct a "create safety" exercise to develop ground rules for group interactions. He begins with Kerth's Prime Directive, a statement that is akin to a ground rule, but that can be used in all retrospectives with teams:

> Regardless of what we discover, we must understand and truly believe that everyone did the best job he or she could, given what was known at the time, his or her skills and abilities, the resources available, and the situation at hand. (Kerth, 2001, p. 7)

He goes on to outline the following exercise for creating safety.

First, begin by stressing that the purpose of the session is to learn and improve rather than to find fault, and that each aspect of the session is optional. That means that no one has to participate if he doesn't feel comfortable doing so. The second step is to take a confidential poll of how safe people feel, especially when their direct supervisors are participating. If appropriate, this is done by secret ballot. The third step involves asking people to form "natural affinity" groups consisting of the people with whom they work most often. Fourth, each group develops a list of ground rules that its members feel would provide them with the safety they need if they are to be comfortable discussing difficult issues without fear of retribution or threat to their careers. Next, these ideas are combined for discussion by the full group. Another poll is then taken to assess the level of safety, assuming that these ground rules are adhered to. Again, this may be done by secret ballot. This process is iterated until members report that they are comfortable moving forward.

In accordance with the core values of effective intervention, ground rules should be freely accepted and agreed to by each group member. When such agreement has been achieved, the rules can always change, yet they provide group members and facilitators with an agreed-upon means of intervening to get a team back on track. When groups have trouble developing their own list of ground rules, the multi-level learning coach can use the models discussed in this chapter to develop an initial list. An example of a "starter list" is given in Table 3.1 and includes the following: Test assumptions and inferences; share all relevant information; focus on interests, not positions; explain the reasoning behind statements; invite questions; stay focused; no cheap shots or jokes at others' expense; do not interrupt while others are speaking; silence is not consent; assume that people did the best they could given the situation they were in; start and end group sessions on time; keep to agreements on prework and follow-ups. You will probably be able to add to this list by drawing on your background and experience in either leading or working with effective teams.

CONCLUSION

The multi-level learning coach is well served by using the core values of effective group intervention: valid information, free and informed choice, and internal commitment to choices. The coach brings a number of skills to her work, including highly effective facilitation, asking questions that generate deeper insight, helping members navigate organizational change, and familiarity with the business and technical context within which her clients work. Although she is not simply a group facilitator, the coach can help teams improve their group process when dysfunction blocks learning and productive reflection. Models of group processes were covered, including effective communication, problem solving, decision making, conflict resolution, and boundary management, so that coaches can make use of the diagnosis-intervention cycle to intervene when required. Establishing agreed-upon ground rules that reflect models of effective group processes enable both the coach and the teams with which he is working

TABLE 3.1
List of Useful Ground Rules

- Test assumptions and inferences
- Share all relevant information
- Focus on interests, not positions
- Explain the reasoning behind statements
- Invite questions
- Stay focused
- No cheap shots

- Limit interruptions
- Silence is not consent
- Assume that people did the best they could given the situation they were in
- Start and end group sessions on time
- Keep to agreements on prework and follow-ups

to keep one another on track and ensure an environment of safety, particularly when discussing difficult or sensitive topics.

In the next chapter, we discuss the role of the project and program management office and the ways in which the leaders of these functions can help to facilitate cross-project learning and continuous improvement.

4 | THE PROJECT AND PROGRAM MANAGEMENT FUNCTION (PMO)

In the previous chapter, we discussed the role of the multi-level learning coach. In this chapter, we discuss the role of the project or program management function, sometimes called a PMO (for project or program management office), but alternatively called a product development group, business transformation group, project services organization, client services group, or center of excellence (Dai, 2002; Engle, 2005; Kerzner, 2006; Rad & Levin, 2002). While a PMO is not required in order to deploy multi-level learning, the functions provided by a PMO can build learning practices into the way work gets done and transfer the resulting improvements from one team to the next.

Victoria Marsick and Karen Watkins (1999) explain that continuous systems-level learning is required if organizations are to improve and transform to achieve higher levels of performance. Their view is based on the work of Chris Argyris and Donald Schön (1996), who view organizational learning as occurring if two criteria are satisfied: (1) individuals, either appointed by management or anointed by followers, "take their learning back to the system," and (2) the system has "structures, processes and a culture in place to embed and support organizational learning" (Marsick & Watkins, 1999, p. 12). Whether they are performed by a PMO or by some other group, the functions of a PMO are important because, as discussed in the previous chapter, people in project environments are continually rotating into and out of roles. When project teams disband upon completion of their work, this often means that "the end of a project is consequently the end of collective learning" (Schindler &

Eppler, 2003). As George Disterer (2002) explains, there is often no "formal corpus" left where existing knowledge can be accessed once projects are over. Because of its temporary nature, project work by itself does not provide the structures necessary to ensure that learning is captured and applied by the organization to improve future project performance (Ekstedt, 1999). Without a knowledge broker or some form of PMO function serving in this capacity, the organization risks losing the knowledge gained by project teams, resulting in redundant work, repetition of mistakes, and considerably higher costs on future projects (Schindler & Eppler, 2003). Effective PMOs are able to "take learning back to the system" and embed the resulting knowledge into the way the organization functions on an ongoing basis. Continuous systems-level learning provides the mechanisms for building learning, knowledge, and adaptation into systems and routines that go beyond the tenure of specific individuals working in the project environment at any one time.

This chapter discusses how leaders of PMOs help their organizations continuously improve their performance from one project and program to the next. The chapter draws on a study of 20 PMO leaders and 6 project managers (Julian, 2008c) from a variety of functional disciplines, including IT (representing the majority, with 65 percent), product development, strategy, finance, and HR, to provide examples of how PMO leaders have helped their organizations build on success and avoid repetition of failure by brokering practice connections across groups and by establishing organizational routines that transfer learning from one project to the next. As we shall also see, however, PMO leaders face a number of obstacles to helping their organizations learn and improve. Many of these obstacles are self-created—and many of them exist because the leaders are stuck in the middle, between trying to manage performance, on the one hand, and serve as facilitators of learning, on the other. We end the chapter with a discussion of how PMOs or similarly structured groups can become more effective brokers of organizational learning and continuous improvement, including how they might work with the multi-level learning coach to overcome many of the obstacles they face.

THE PMO

PMOs originated in the middle of the twentieth century, when the defense industry needed to coordinate large, complex contracts that included many projects for a single large customer (Kerzner, 2006). PMOs have since evolved into a variety of different forms, yet they are typically staffed with full-time members who "provide some combination of managerial, administrative, training, consulting and technical services for projects and the organization overall" (Dai, 2002, p. 26). The PMO provides a focal point for the discipline of project management, in some cases taking on direct responsibility for managing projects, and in other cases providing consultative or administrative services to project managers, project teams, and/or senior management (Dai, 2002; Kerzner, 2004; Rad & Levin, 2002).

The impetus for introducing PMOs is often to improve project management performance and to reduce the number of "runaway" projects—those that fail to meet customer expectations, run over budget, or become compromisingly delayed (Stanleigh, 2006). Jerry Julian (2008a) found, for example, that continuous improvement was often an explicit responsibility of many of the 20 PMO leaders participating in his study. Parvis Rad and Ginger Levin (2002) describe PMOs as providing support at both the project level and the management level. Although each organization implements PMOs in different ways, support at the project level is provided through training, consulting, and mentoring of project personnel. At the management level, PMOs support continuous improvement by "archiving project performance data, compiling lessons learned, establishing knowledge management systems, and developing checklists and tools for standardized project management processes" (Rad & Levin, p. 3).

C. X. Dai and W. G. Wells (2004) conducted a survey of 209 PMO organizations to investigate the relationship between PMO presence and project performance. They found that the presence of certain PMO functions—particularly the ongoing establishment and reinforcement of project management standards and methods—was correlated with increased project success. They also found that some PMOs report to senior levels of management at the divisional or company level, while others report to specific functional leaders (i.e., finance, human resources, or information technology).

H. Kerzner (2004) claims that the concept of the PMO "could very well be the most important project management activity in this decade" (p. 379). The promises of PMOs include standardization of the project management process, better resource utilization, more effective prioritization of work, and the development of future project managers (Kerzner, 2006). Rad and Levin claim that the trend toward implementing PMOs in organizations will only continue as projects become "a way of life for more and more organizations" (2002, p. 1).

BROKERING AND COMMUNITIES OF PRACTICE

In the previous chapter, we introduced the concept of communities of practice—groups of people who share a concern, a set of problems, or a passion about a topic, and who deepen their knowledge and expertise in this area by interacting on an ongoing basis, developing their own shared history, artifacts, and ways of solving problems in the process. Management groups represent one form of a community of practice. Companies like GE, Procter & Gamble, and Pepsi are well known for their pervasive management cultures. People in specific departments performing similar work—software developers, for example—may also develop their own community of practice. Likewise, people with specific interests from various areas in organizations may also develop a community of practice. Project managers in different functions, for example, may get together to share best practices and develop new tools, techniques, and processes for doing project work, even though they don't work together on a routine basis otherwise (for those readers who are interested, Appendix B provides a complete overview of theories of situated learning and communities of practice). Organizations are, in effect, a constellation of these types of communities of practice (Wenger, 1998).

In the previous chapter, we also talked about the role that brokers (people who span multiple communities of practice) play and how they provide translation, alignment, and coordination between perspectives to combine multiple practices in ways that can enable learning and innovation. Members of cross-functional teams, for example, play a brokering role, as each member comes from his own community of practice and combines his perspectives with those of others. It may even be possible, with sufficient time and continuity, for a project team to develop its own

routines and norms in ways that make it resemble a community of practice, even though the members of cross-functional teams come from a
diverse array of communities themselves.

Perhaps more so than anyone else, PMO leaders sit squarely in the role
of a broker. They span at least two and possibly more communities: upper
management, project teams, and the PMO group, staffed as it is with its
own personnel. They may also work with groups of vendors, suppliers,
and customers, serving as the "glue" that enables strategies, programs,
processes, and projects to work together effectively. As will be described
later in the chapter, they facilitate learning from past project experiences
for the benefit of current and future projects by brokering practice connections between management, project teams, and other communities of
practice (Julian, 2008a).

RESEARCH METHODOLOGY

As mentioned previously, this chapter draws on a study of PMO leaders
and project managers (Julian, 2008c) to shed light on how PMO leaders facilitate cross-project learning and continuous improvement. The
study includes 20 PMO leaders and 6 project managers from a variety of
industries, including healthcare, financial services, consumer products,
software, management consulting, and airline transport, although a
majority (65%) worked within the information technology setting. The
functional domains in which the PMO leaders worked include information technology, product development, finance, and human resources.
Others served the strategic needs of their organization across all of these
domains. An approximately equal percentage of men and women were
represented.

Participants were interviewed for approximately 60 minutes each.
Data from the interviews were transcribed and coded. After findings were
compiled from the PMO leader interviews, a focus group consisting of
six project managers who had reported to PMO leaders in the past was
conducted. Project managers represent "the next level down" on the organization chart in PMO environments. The aim of the project manager
focus group was to provide an additional point of triangulation of the
PMO leaders' perspectives. The project managers in this group were not

interviewed individually and represent a different participant population than the PMO leaders.

Finally, a summative focus group was conducted with six PMO leaders who had been interviewed in order to confirm and elaborate the interview findings. This group, having participated in the interview process, represented a different population than the first focus group, which consisted of project managers who had reported to PMO leaders on past assignments.

HOW PMO LEADERS FACILITATE CROSS-PROJECT LEARNING AND CONTINUOUS IMPROVEMENT

This section draws on the findings of the above study, to describe how PMO leaders facilitate cross-project learning and continuous improvement. To provide a bridge from theory to practice for the reader, Table 4.1 lists a number of learning theory–based categories (described in Appendix B), along with examples that provide a translation from the conceptual to the practical—that is, how the behaviors are manifested in actual practice.

TABLE 4.1
Theoretical Categories and Their Manifestations in Practice

Theoretical Category	Manifestation in Practice
Brokering	The PMO leader coordinates and aligns groups, departments, and teams, translating their community-specific languages and ideas in order to facilitate project-related communication.
Boundary encounter	An ad hoc or nonroutine meeting with members of two or more groups, teams, or departments.
Boundary practice	An ongoing process established by the PMO to facilitate alignment among management, project teams, and the PMO. Examples include status reporting, lessons-learned sessions, and face-to-face knowledge sharing.
Boundary objects	Tools, templates, intranet portals, and databases that facilitate knowledge capture and exchange.
Reflective practices	Often manifested as organizational members discussing "what worked and what didn't" with respect to past project experiences or PMO processes.

FIGURE 4.1
Sample Characteristics

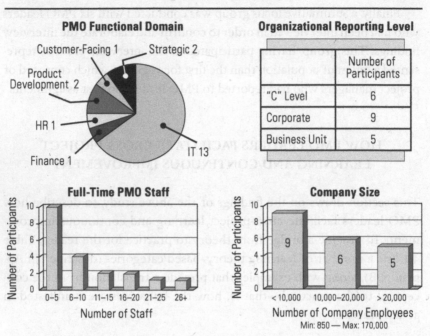

PMO Functional Domain

Customer-Facing 1   Strategic 2
Product Development 2
HR 1
Finance 1
IT 13

Organizational Reporting Level

	Number of Participants
"C" Level	6
Corporate	9
Business Unit	5

Full-Time PMO Staff

Number of Participants — 0–5, 6–10, 11–15, 16–20, 21–25, 26+
Number of Staff

Company Size

Number of Participants — 9 (<10,000), 6 (10,000–20,000), 5 (>20,000)
Number of Company Employees
Min: 850 — Max: 170,000

Figure 4.1 shows the characteristics of the sample in the PMO leader study, while Table 4.2 provides a summary of the findings. A discussion of each of these findings follows, including representative quotations from participants. All names used are pseudonyms to ensure the confidentiality of the participants and their organizations.

Brokering

All 20 participants indicated that they create practice connections between project teams and management, providing coordination, alignment, or translation between and among these communities in order to facilitate learning from past project experiences.

Coordination. The vast majority (90 percent) of the PMO leaders indicated that they helped their organizations learn from past project experiences by coordinating practice connections. Patty talked about how she and her

TABLE 4.2
Overview of PMO Leader Brokering Study Findings (Julian, 2008c)

All the PMO leaders facilitated learning from past project experiences for the benefit of current and future projects by brokering practice connections between management, project teams, and other communities of practice.

Brokering:
- All participants indicated that they create practice connections between project teams and management, providing coordination, alignment, or translation between and among these communities.

Boundary practices:
- All participants expressed that they had established processes that are common to multiple projects—including lessons-learned practices, project methodologies, and status reporting and governance processes—that bring opportunities for learning to the surface and provide a vehicle for transferring lessons learned to current and future projects.

Boundary objects:
- All participants expressed using tools and templates, systems, or documents that provide a means for incorporating learning from past project experiences into future projects.

Boundary encounters:
- The vast majority of the PMO leaders (85 percent) reported that they and/or their staff coordinated boundary encounters in order to (1) intervene with project teams to diagnose and remediate project-related problems, (2) transfer project management standards to new teams, or (3) continuously improve project management processes.

Reflective practices:
- Three-quarters of the participants described how they engage in content and/or process reflection to diagnose project-related problems and to help stakeholders learn from past project experiences.

Formal training:
- Just under half (45 percent) of the participants reported that they provide formal training in project management to transfer lessons learned, including project methodologies and "soft skills" that are deemed important to the organization.

Personal experience as project manager:
- Less than half (40 percent) of the participants indicated that they or their staff drew upon their personal experiences as a project manager to determine where improvements needed to be made.

Personnel selection:
- A few (15 percent) of the participants reported that they transfer lessons learned from past project experiences by selecting future project managers with the requisite competencies.

team coordinated one such learning process that involved multiple project managers using previously documented lessons learned:

> Again, we scour and go through the project closing documents for each project that closed for that year, and we identify on our own within the PMO what we believe to be the nuggets. Then what we will do is we will reach out to a select number of project managers, who were re-

sponsible for those projects, work with them to develop presentations for their peers, and then we will hold a formal lessons-learned workshop with this audience.

June described how she and her team coordinated a project kickoff where they transferred lessons learned from previous failures by providing clear roles and responsibilities up front, so that all participants would know what to expect from one another:

So when you invite eight people to be part of a particular work stream, what role is each one of them playing? So that when we kick off the project (and we actually just did this with a project that's kicking off next week), every single person walks in saying, "I'm here to listen and provide input, but I've got no decision rights here." Or, "I'm being asked to build this, and these are the people to whom I need to listen." You know, it's sort of an obvious thing, but we're making it incredibly explicit.

Alignment. The vast majority of the participants (85 percent) also reported brokering activities related to aligning the perspectives of two or more communities by addressing conflicts, particularly when problems arose at the project level. Through these interventions, PMO leaders were able to bring to the surface issues from past project experiences that needed to be addressed, often in order to maintain alignment between project teams and senior management. June talked about her experience working with a project team that management felt was running off course:

So what we did was we pulled the operating committee, in fact, we pulled three operating committee members together with their direct reports that were involved in this, and sort of went back a couple of steps and then went through the assumption process; identified why this disconnect seemed to be happening, in terms of what they thought we were asking them to do versus what we were actually asking them to do. We reconfirmed that it was okay to go forward, documented it, and then moved from there.

Victor described how he facilitated alignment by working with senior management to implement new project methodologies that were based on his previous experience as a project manager:

What I did was I got buy-in from the management level on both the business and IT sides with my boss and my peers, in terms of some of the things I was recommending, and also I would take any feedback that they provided me and obviously try to apply it in some way, shape, or form, if I thought it was justified. So I basically, in this case, kind of did a top-down approach, in terms of getting the buy-in from the management staff before rolling it out to kind of the team leader level staff.

In the summative focus group consisting of a subset of the PMO leaders interviewed, Suzie confirmed the importance of coordination and alignment within her context:

So in our case, I would say the majority of our activities are around co-ordination and kind of connecting the dots. Most of the activity we've done so far is more around program management, where we're trying to help align a larger program and multiple project managers within that program. So definitely alignment and coordination have been our top activities so far.

Translation. Most of the participants (70 percent) also report engaging in activities related to translating one community's meanings into the language of another community in order to facilitate the learning process between them. Patty's previous quote demonstrates how her team "scours" the database to uncover "nuggets" that should be shared with other project managers. Antonio described another such translation activity in which he facilitated engagement between a project team and senior management:

Now I should say that prior to these PMO meetings, I obtained the business case summary, the financial model that they've put together for these projects. And I provide a very high level pre-read copy for the PMO committee at least a week in advance of the meeting. So that they're not going in cold to those meetings.

In the summative focus group, Robert talked about a $50,000 project he launched specifically to help one community—the information technology department—understand the language and practices of "the business community" by publishing a "black book":

> We have the IT department of like, at the time, 300 people. And we had a business community that was suspicious of the IT department's understanding of the business and how it actually functions and how it actually makes money. That suspicion led to a credibility issue. So there was a chasm between what technology could enable for the business community and what the business community thought technology could enable for them. So to address that chasm, we said, "You know what? Maybe IT doesn't understand the business. Let's write a book about the business and give it out to everybody in IT." And the code name for the book was called the Black Book. And it was the who, what, where, when of how we make money.

Boundary Practices

All participants stated that they had established processes that are common to multiple projects—including lessons-learned practices, project methodologies, and status reporting and governance processes—that bring opportunities for learning to the surface and provide a vehicle for transferring lessons learned to current and future projects.

Lessons-Learned Practices. Lessons-learned practices were the most common boundary practice that brought opportunities for learning to the surface. The great majority of the participants (85 percent) reported that they or their company require project teams to conduct lessons-learned sessions upon project closure, resulting in a "lessons-learned document." The purpose of the lessons-learned sessions was to encourage team members to reflect on their past project experiences in order to identify opportunities for improvement on future projects. Robert described how lessons learned were required by his PMO after projects were completed:

> And as a PMO, we insist upon a lessons learned or a postmortem after every project. About two weeks after every project, there has to be a lessons learned, a postmortem. We follow a fairly standard template, pretty robust. It's not a witch hunt. It's a, "What went well? What could have gone better?"

Robert also described how he required project managers who were participating in lessons-learned sessions to seek out others who might benefit from the resulting knowledge:

Anything that we can take from that and immediately apply to other projects, one or more other projects, the project manager usually contacts the other gaining project manager, if you will. The one that's gaining the knowledge from this lessons learned and says, "Hey, be on the lookout for something like this. It hasn't happened in a while, but it just happened on my project."

In answering a question in the project manager focus group about how PMOs help project teams learn from past project experiences, one project manager confirmed the existence of lessons-learned practices in her environment, saying, "One of the processes that we put in place at my last company was that [a lessons-learned document] was a required deliverable before you could exit a project."

Status Reporting and Governance.   The great majority of the PMO leaders (85 percent) have established status reporting and project governance practices that bring opportunities for learning from past project experiences to the surface. Rachel explained her PMO's approach to status reporting and its focus on uncovering problem areas that might have emerged over the course of a project's life cycle:

That takes us right back to those project updates. In terms of, once a month, formally the project managers are reporting out along a lot of different areas. Actually one point I want to make is, over the year, we've also refined what they're reporting out on so that it's not just a red-amber-green rating on the overall project. But we've asked for more granularity. Maybe the overall project is amber, but where are you green? Where are you red? Where are you yellow? Is it around financials? Controls? Project planning? Resource management? You know, so forth, and so on. So that's another lessons learned, not just to broad sweep a project red, yellow, or green, but in fact try to focus in on the root cause.

Sarah described a jolting experience resulting from a senior executive's "no-go" decision caused by a project governance checkpoint, an event that spurred efforts to reflect on the reasons why the mission-critical project had faltered:

> I found out through a report from the project manager and the head of the London office, to say that the key deliverable for that phase with a "go/no-go" had been called a "no-go." Then there was a plea for help, which is, "What do we do?"—You know, "This calls into question everything now. Our plans, our resources. What are we going to do?" So that's how I found out.

Cathy described how she is moving toward establishing a more formal governance process that involves senior decision makers, ensuring alignment between business priorities and project management:

> What we're trying to do right now is we're putting in a set of gates. So that you have to pass through certain gates, which will be certain evaluations. We do this now informally, and a lot of the projects go through this, but we're trying to make it so that they all go through this and no one bypasses it because we really want to have everything aligned with the business objectives, and we want to make sure that there are other VPs, especially on the business side, who are aware of what's being requested and are aware of what's going on.

In response to the finding that PMO project governance triggers learning opportunities, as in Sarah's and Cathy's situations, one of the project managers said the following in the project manager focus group:

> Well, I think who you're presenting to . . . the members of the steering committee often have good questions or key points that help to reflect a little bit more on how the project is being conducted. I mean, it's not the best place to learn but . . . it happens. (Project Manager 3)

In a discussion of the ways in which PMO leaders transfer learning in the summative focus group, Rachel confirmed the role that status reporting and governance can play:

> You know, we use the tollgate concept, where basically you have to present certain documents, so you can get through the tollgate and that helps [to ensure learning is transferred to future projects].

Project Methodologies.   Project methodologies were clearly the most common boundary practice that made past learning available to future projects. Most participants (80 percent) had established guidelines for project managers that outline requirements, standards, or guidelines for managing project work that were intended to incorporate lessons from past project experiences. Mitch described how his firm has incorporated improvements into its project methodology based on past project experiences:

> The other piece is that, you know, where we have learned clearly from the past, and brought forward into future projects are things like a— more of the acceptance criteria for our vendors. In other words, there are some acceptance criteria that we have written from our vendors when they hand us something. "Okay, we're not going to take it unless you have this, this, and this done." So those are things that we have learned, as we've moved forward and brought into future projects what we've done.

Rachel talked about another example of incorporating previous learning into a project methodology:

> Another area of lessons learned is having a documented communications plan, change management plans. So you know, all the good practices, but just making them more and more—I don't like using the word "formal"—but more and more expected. As part of your role as a PM, you have to have these things in place.

Knowledge-Sharing Forums.   Half the PMO leaders (50 percent) reported that they had established knowledge-sharing sessions at which project managers or PMO staff share lessons learned, providing others with an opportunity to learn from their experiences. Wendy described one such example of an informal face-to-face knowledge-sharing session where project managers got together for lunch:

> Every month, I sponsor the "Lunch and Learn," where I have like all 30 employees and consultants in the tank, and that's where I'd get an hour and a half with them. And in there, we would talk about lessons learned as well. We have a chance for the PM to say what's working well and what is not working well.

Patty discussed another example of face-to-face knowledge sharing where her staff members, consisting of project "liaisons" that maintain connections with project managers and project teams, meet to discuss current issues and identify learning opportunities:

> The members of the PMO have weekly team meetings. Through those weekly team meetings, we will do liaison updates that help to promote and identify things that are happening out there, as real time as possible, that will be headline-worthy, newsworthy, action-oriented for the PMO as a whole, or to further equip or better equip our PMO liaisons in the liaison role. So we really kind of do this as an iterative process all the time, depending on what the real-life issues or things are. So the PMO, in a way, doesn't wait every year for the lessons-learned activity at a formal level to occur before we identify opportunities to address things as we see them.

One of the project managers in the project manager focus group talked about his experience with knowledge-sharing forums in which very specific lessons learned were selected and discussed among project managers:

> Another thing is, like we have, what do you call it? A monthly meeting, all heads meet to do the Project of the Month. . . . So basically what we do is we pick up something special about a project. . . . We pick up a very specific situation. Okay, we reached a problem, a typical problem situation within the scope of the program. . . . We concentrate on that pertinent piece [versus] the whole project because we have realized that we do not get that kind of attention when you're talking about the whole project. (Project Manager 1)

Boundary Objects

All the participants reported using tools and templates, systems, or documents that provide a means of incorporating learning from past project experiences into future projects.

Tools and templates were utilized by 85 percent of participants to share and transfer learning from past project experiences. Wendy described how she and her team developed a standard template and refined it as they learned more over the course of their project experiences:

So we have a document that outlines all of the product information needed to actually build a product. Then it becomes the product record, so to speak. So that the next time the product needs to be upgraded or modified, you can go back to that sort of source document and then work from there to do your change estimates and figure out what needs to be done. We've been fine-tuning that document. I mean we were fine-tuning it basically weekly for the first couple of months we used it.

In response to the question, "What are some other ways in which PMOs transfer learning?" a project manager similarly talked about the role of tools in his PMO experience:

They can share tools that worked on one project for another project. And also the ability to use Microsoft Project. Because Microsoft Project has many, many different ways of using it, with tools and views and whatever. It's not really standardizing it, but by using it the same way, you can give some knowledge from previous projects of things that work and things that didn't work, moving on to the next project.

Systems such as intranet portals, databases, and project tracking tools were also utilized by 65 percent of the PMO leaders to share or transfer learning from past project experiences. Rachel described how her team established an intranet site to share tools and templates:

We put up a site to house the various templates and examples of— you know, not magic, but actually put up a project management site so people could find these templates, and find the charter document, and find an example, and find a communication plan. Because there was this endless, like, "Oh, can you send me—Can you send me?" And then you're searching through e-mails. So just that is a simple way of helping people with the tools.

Similarly, Cathy described how her team posts status reports to the intranet so that others in the organization can see what projects are currently in progress along with their current status:

But the status reports are out there on the intranet web site that anyone can reference any time. So we're trying to keep them current. I do take snapshots (like I freeze the dashboard), and I have historical information. But what's out there, like if you were to go on our web site and click on a particular project, you would be able to see the current status of that project.

The use of documents to facilitate learning from past project experiences was reported by 40 percent of the PMO leaders. Documents were used when tools or templates for the particular purpose at hand were not available. Mitch, for example, documented a lesson learned in order to ensure that a vendor, an outside company, was provided with formal written notice regarding his company's expectations for the future when and if a similar problem occurred: "What we did was we documented [the lesson learned] and are now working with our vendor to make sure that when we are working with something that involves both parts of their company, that those parts are communicating adequately." Similarly, Victor described how he used a slide deck to capture the collective learning of a project team after a lessons-learned session so that it could be forwarded to others:

It does get documented. We prepare a slide deck, usually about 10 slides, that includes kind of everything that happened on the [most recent phase of the project], including what scope was delivered; what scope might we have deferred that we were planning to deliver; how many hours of work were completed, etc., etc.; and then we kind of say—there's a slide for what worked well; what did not work well. We review that as a management team, and make any adjustments we feel are necessary, not just to the team that produced the feedback, but making sure that other teams taking a similar approach also get that same feedback.

Boundary Encounters

The vast majority of the PMO leaders (85 percent) reported that they and/ or their staff coordinated boundary encounters in order to (1) intervene with project teams to diagnose and remediate project-related problems, (2) transfer project management standards to new teams, or (3) continuously improve project management processes.

Project Intervention. Just over half (55 percent) of the PMO leaders indicated that they held discussions with key project or management personnel in order to diagnose and remediate problems occurring at the project level. June described how she worked with one of her project managers to better understand what was happening with a project team that began to falter:

> I think, the project manager that kicked off the project and I sat down and went through, "Okay, this is what we're hearing. This is what it looks like. What is causing this?" We did a little bit of sort of informal cause analysis and came to the conclusion that where people thought that others had agreed to move forward, they actually hadn't yet. Then we went back and sort of researched it to see if that was true, and it seemed to be true.

Similarly, Melissa described how she engaged a project team to help improve its project delivery practices:

> So I attended their meetings. In fact, [my boss] had me start running their team meetings, to figure out what they were doing. . . . So I was meeting with them combined as well, putting stuff in place for them, standards and things. So that's how I got into that one.

Transfer of Standards. Some of the PMO leaders (35 percent) reported that they or their staff met with others in the project environment, including project managers, project teams, or senior management, in order to transfer previously established lessons and standards to future project efforts. Patty described how she engaged the executive team in spreading the word about lessons learned from the previous year's project work:

> So much of what happens gets derived out of the lessons learned at the project team level. It gets bundled up, and it gets incorporated into— it's an annual executive training, where we get airtime every year in front of all of our executives. It's typically our directors and above, and the project management office has carte blanche to identify and decide, "What is the most pertinent project management topic, or lesson, to be given to executives?"

Similarly, Seth talked about how he transferred improved practices to an existing project that looked very similar to two massive failures for which he had previously developed two case studies:

And this was during the time that we were evaluating what'd taken place on these first two deals that I had mentioned to you. And she said, you know, she threw up a flag, to her credit, and said, "Help. Somebody's got to come look at this, because this could unravel." And we did and said, "You're right, and this has all the earmarks of what we just looked at." Even though the director position was not funded in anybody's budget, we said, "The right thing to do is to put the fix in before we encounter the problem." So we put the person in there.

The development and dissemination of the two case studies that Seth had coordinated enabled others in the organization to understand some of the pitfalls that large, multi-business-unit projects entailed. He was subsequently able to leverage the learning from these two prior failures by aligning the troubled project with new practices aimed at preventing the past failures from recurring.

Process Improvement.   Some of the PMO leaders (30 percent) coordinated delegations from various groups in attempts to implement improvements in the organization's project management processes. June described the quarterly meetings she hosts to improve the organization's project management methodology:

It starts with, you know, compared to last quarter—"What did you think went easier this time than it did last time? What are the things that seem to be recurring? Here's the list of issues we identified last quarter; have any of them actually gone away? And/or do you see any of these still here and/or getting worse?" And then we'll delve into the things that seem—and the things that got better, we also talk about why we think they got better.

Similarly, Greg discussed how he coordinated an encounter with a key department in which they reflected on their partnership in order to improve their collaborative process:

I proposed, and it was very well received, that we have a workshop, where we bring ourselves together and we talk about, "How can we leverage ourselves to be more successful? How can we maximize the effectiveness of the partnership?" And that was all about looking at where the partnerships are working really well, what can we learn from that and transmit it to the rest of the organization.

Reflective Practices

Three-quarters of the PMO leaders described how they engage in content and/or process reflection (Mezirow, 1991) to diagnose project-related problems or improve processes that are common to multiple projects. As discussed in Chapter 2, content reflection involves reviewing how ideas have been applied at each stage of a problem-solving process or over the course of a project. The second form of reflection, process reflection, examines the problem-solving process itself, focusing on the procedures and assumptions involved in process standards and methodologies that apply to multiple projects.

Content Reflection.   Almost half of the PMO leaders (50 percent) declared that they engaged in content reflection. Mack described how he engaged project members in content reflection by polling project members individually prior to a lessons-learned session with a project team:

> One way, which I like the most, is to ask everybody to, which I've been recommending to project managers, you know, to send an e-mail to everybody on the team, asking them to write a couple of things. What went well and what went wrong? What could we have improved? And send it back to me or whoever is the PM. In that case, what happens is one person cannot influence the others. So we just get all the feedback and somebody synthesizes that data and then presents it in front of the team together.

Similarly, Suzie described how she polled project members before a meeting she called to get a troubled project team back on track:

> What I did before the meeting, just to make sure I really understood everything, is I went around to each person that had been involved

and I asked them about the project: where it was; what were the challenges; what might be the hurdles to success; what difficulties they were having.

Process Reflection. Process reflection was reported by just under half (45 percent) of the PMO leaders. June described how her team engaged in process reflection to improve her product development approach after completing a series of recent product development projects:

> We had done our fourth set of postmortems on releases. Right? So we get together as a team and we say, "Okay. What happened this time? What was really good this time? What wasn't so good, etc., etc.?" And what we realized was three quarters in a row, we were having role and responsibility issues and decision right issues, and one of the root causes was organizational change. So what we realized was, "Is there a way to sort of codify at a point in time what we're asking someone to do?"

Similarly, Patty described how her team reflected on its processes in order to continuously improve:

> And we did an actual lessons learned, if you will, of the process that we had initially designed and developed, which includes a three-phase process on how we nominate, prioritize, and select portfolio items. And then we'll go through an end-to-end evaluation to identify opportunities to streamline, be more efficient, and articulate better results.

Formal Training

Of the PMO leaders in this study, 45 percent indicated that they provide formal training in project management that enables lessons learned or "best practices" to be shared or transferred, including project methodologies and "soft skills" that are deemed to be important within the organization. Classroom training of this sort is made available to project managers, team members, and in some cases senior executives. Debra described how her organization, in conjunction with the training group, rolled out a new project management training program for executives:

Actually, we also offer, I'm going to call it like a—the Fire Hose Project Management Class for Executives. We call it "Just Enough Project Management," so we offer that, so that we're hitting all the levels. From an executive's perspective, "What are some of the things I need to be looking for in order to help project managers run projects for my organizations? What are some of the areas I can assist?" We actually give them a laminated card with the phases of a project, and it's all PMI-compliant. What are the phases? And then what are the questions they should be asking when they're in a specific phase?

Similarly, Cathy described how her organization rolled out training for project members:

We have a certain group that provides training, that we've contracted, that has actually—you can take how to run projects from a pure state, and then you can also put the Consumerco pieces into that training. And that's what this particular organization was able to do. The head of the training was able to make that connection with them and to have it customized so that not only did you get the theory, but you actually got a lot of the practical sides of the pieces that we require here at Consumerco.

Personal Experience as Project Manager

Almost half the PMO leaders (40 percent) reported that they either had learned from past project experiences themselves or had staff members who drew on their own experiences as former project managers within the same organization. These personal experiences as project managers within the organization were perceived to have shaped their thinking about areas that needed improvement. Harold talked about how he drew on his previous experience as a project manager within his organization to develop ideas for improvement, saying, "Part of getting this job was I took a lot of my experiences as a PM and said, here's the things we need to work at from a PM's perspective." Debra explained how one member of her staff had similarly drawn on his experience as a project manager to document lessons learned in order to improve future projects:

His first job here was as an infrastructure project manager. So it was the knowledge base, and let's share that knowledge and let's get it out there so that people are not reinventing the wheel over and over and over. So there, the lessons learned were basically documented and put into a process.

Personnel Selection

A few (15 percent) of the PMO leaders transferred lessons from past project experiences by selecting future project managers with the requisite competencies. Sarah's team, for example, after having the "plug pulled" on a project before it went live, held a lessons-learned session after the project was finally over. As a result of that meeting, she and her peer, who manages the "technical managers," decided not to place people in that role as project managers in the future. She explained this scenario as follows:

So he and I decided that, as a direct lesson from Australia, remembering that very, very, very well, and others, that we would make it immediate policy that no technical manager was allowed to be a project manager anymore.

June, after "rescuing" a faltering project, determined that in the future, project managers would have to have a certain mind-set, one that the previous project manager had not had:

And what's happened is that person is not engaged any longer in those sorts of projects because this is not a person who is good at anticipating obstacles and planning for them. What's required in that role is what I call "optimistic half-empty thinking."

ENABLERS AND BARRIERS THAT PMO LEADERS FACE IN FACILITATING CROSS-PROJECT LEARNING AND CONTINUOUS IMPROVEMENT

The PMO leaders in the study described in this chapter were asked to discuss "critical incidents"—high points or low points—where they either attempted to help their organization learn from a past project experience or attempted to share or transfer that learning to other projects within their organization. Two additional interview questions were also asked: The first was, "In what ways does the organization support your efforts to learn from project work and/or share lessons learned with your team and others?" And the second was, "If you were given the authority, what would you do in the organization to make it easier to learn from project work and share lessons learned with your team and others?" Both of these questions, in combination with the critical incident discussions, generated a multiplicity of barriers and enablers of cross-project learning. A summary of these barriers and enablers is presented in Table 4.3. As in the previous section, a discussion of each of these findings follows, along with representative quotes.

Enablers of Cross-Project Learning and Improvement

One of the two most frequently occurring enablers of cross-project learning mentioned by PMO leaders was the quality of their relationships with others, particularly those over whom they have limited direct authority, including project team members, project managers, senior managers, and others coming in and out of the project environment.

Network of Strong Relationships. A majority of the PMO leaders (60 percent) stated that they were able to facilitate cross-project learning because of the quality and/or quantity of good relationships that they had established across their organization. For example, Patty described how her close relationship with the senior management team enabled her and her group to fulfill their responsibilities more effectively:

> I have a seat at the senior executive table, and as such, I'm involved in all the strategy, all the discussion of what's going on, and have that unique ability to knit the 30,000-foot view to the 3,000-foot view to the 3-foot view. And as a result of having 360-degree observation of the organization and a firm pulse across all levels, it's the only way that you're going to be able to have some of the stuff be identified, and address it in a way in which it's going to be a value to the organization.

TABLE 4.3
Perceived Enablers and Barriers to Cross-Project Learning and Continuous Improvement

Enablers

The majority of PMO leaders identified a network of strong relationships and support from senior management as enablers of learning from past project experiences. Other enablers include a learning-oriented culture, a neutral facilitator for lessons learned, and professional development.

- Over half (60%) of the participants expressed a network of strong relationships as an enabler of cross-project learning.
- Over half (60%) of the participants also reported support from senior management as a key enabler.
- A third (30%) of the participants expressed that their organization's culture also plays a positive role in facilitating cross-project learning.
- A quarter (25%) of the participants also noted the following enablers:
  - Utilizing a "neutral" facilitator for lessons-learned sessions.
  - Developing the professional capabilities of project managers through training, apprenticeship, or knowledge-sharing.
- One-tenth (10%) of the participants expressed reflection throughout the project as an enabler rather than only upon project closure.

Barriers

The majority of PMO leaders identified a lack of direct influence over project managers and/or teams as a barrier to learning from past project experiences. Other barriers include staff rotation, fear of airing mistakes publicly, deferring reflection until the end of projects, and difficulty accessing prior lessons learned.

- Just over half (55%) of participants pointed to a lack of direct authority over project managers or project teams as a major barrier to continuously improving upon past project experiences.
- Just under half (45%) of participants noted time pressures and resistance to the "extra work" required of PMO processes as a barrier to cross-project learning.
- Just under half (45%) of participants also identified staff rotation as a barrier to cross-project learning.
- Just over a third (35%) of participants expressed that team members may fear airing mistakes publicly, making it difficult to learn from past project experiences.
- A few (20%) of the participants also noted the following barriers to cross-project learning:
  - Reflection is often deferred until the end of the project.
  - Lack of senior management support.
  - Organizational members' difficulty accessing past lessons learned.

Similarly, Cathy explained how her personal network in combination with her role in the PMO helps her to learn about problems "on the ground":

I think I've been here enough, I guess I'm social enough that I have certain networks, that people feel open, that they can come to me and talk to me about different situations. You know, an individual tower manager or a director in a certain area wouldn't be looking over across the whole organization, whereas the PMO is. So they would come here.

Senior Management Support. A majority of the participants (60 percent) also reported that senior management support is a key enabler of their ability to facilitate learning and continuous improvement. Victor described how support from his senior leadership helped him to gain buy-in from project teams in conducting postmortems:

> You know, once they've implemented, now they've got to do some sort of postmortem work? It's a lot of energy and effort on their part. So to have the senior leadership team accept that and sort of support it, knowing that it's going to cause additional work for the project teams, once the project's done, I think it's a good indication that they see value in making sure that we have post-implementation reviews.

Similarly, Wendy talked about the importance of having a senior "champion" and how it helped her establish more credibility for the PMO:

> He would basically make decisions happen where they wouldn't have if I didn't have his sponsorship. I don't know if you've worked in a large organization, but if you don't have that Godfather, you could be waiting till the cows come home. Because it's a greatest idea, but if no one listens, it doesn't really matter. So really decision making, visibility. I mean he actually championed me all the way up to the chairman of the organization, which was really nice, for the PMO, the credibility of the PMO, but also for myself professionally. You know? So that's kind of how we promoted the PMO, because he believed in us.

In response to questions about how her group overcomes the problems associated with a lack of direct authority, one PMO leader in the summative focus group explained the key supporting role that "project sponsors" and other senior managers have played in her efforts to facilitate cross-project learning:

> Well, that's where we really rely on the sponsors, the management team members who act as sponsors, to be advocates for the PMO

process. Otherwise just having a PMO with senior folks who really aren't that interested in it, definitely didn't work for us. So the idea of— you know, our steering committees always have senior management on them who are well aware of the process we want to follow around tollgates or certain documents or go/no-go decisions.

Learning-Oriented Culture. Some of the PMO leaders (30 percent) indicated that their organization's "way of doing business" plays an enabling role in their efforts to facilitate cross-project learning. Rachel, for example, discussed how, after three years of evolution in the PMO, her organization has developed a culture that favors continuous learning:

> The only thing I would say is that we always do [lessons learned]. So I don't want to overplay that there was this one bad project and we had to take a step back. I think as good project managers, and given the structure we've put in place, you don't wait. There's no ceremony. It's just, "Let's keep looking at what's going right or wrong here and making sure we're adjusting course."

Similarly, Mitch described how his organization's culture also enabled learning to occur routinely:

> [Lessons-learned practices] are culturally engrained. We've been doing those for years, whether it's on projects, other things, do well/do better is a cultural norm for us, so there were really no barriers there.

Neutral Facilitator for Lessons-Learned Sessions. One-quarter of the PMO leaders talked about how having a "neutral facilitator" for lessons-learned sessions helps to promote a more productive discussion. For some of the participants, this meant having someone other than the project manager facilitate the lessons-learned session. For others, it meant ensuring that the process was run in a fair manner, focusing less on blame and more on planning how to prevent the problem from recurring. In some cases, the PMO considered itself more "neutral" and therefore saw itself as being in a better position to conduct the exercise, and in other cases, an outside party, possibly a project manager from another team, would be brought in to perform this function. Patty described in detail how her PMO staff not only facilitates the lessons-learned workshop, but also attempts to create an environment conducive to fostering productive dialogue:

> Because one of the things that we think is very valuable and beneficial to the organization as a whole is the fact that we are probably the one neutral department in the organization that doesn't own a piece of the business in any way, shape, or form. . . . I think the key is the facilitation of the lessons-learned workshop. That's one of the reasons why we tend to put a PMO liaison in that role, rather than the PM. We make sure that there are ground rules established at the beginning of each lessons-learned workshop, focusing on and emphasizing the need for honest feedback, declaring up front that the feedback that may be received isn't personal; that we try to keep a limit to our criticisms at a constructive level. And ideally, the recommendations or the output from the lessons-learned workshop shouldn't just be complaints, but it should be actionable.

Likewise, one of the project managers in the project manager focus group talked about how he emphasizes "the process," not "the people," in his lessons-learned sessions:

> When we do lessons learned, we talk about some of the situations, what worked and what did not work. If it's emphasizing the person, then it becomes counterproductive. But if we emphasize the process . . . that's how we try to make it a more beneficial process for all of us.

Another one of the project managers confirmed the need for effective facilitation, saying, "Yeah. It's like emphasizing the positive and not the negative. Because the tendency is to emphasize, especially in postmortems—it becomes a 'blamestorming' more than anything else."

Professional Development. One-quarter of the PMO leaders also pointed to professional development as an enabler of cross-project learning. Professional development activities facilitated project learning in a number of ways. In one case, training was provided that equipped staff members with the skills required to conduct productive lessons-learned sessions. In another case, the organization required that each project member attain a certain number of professional development "credits" as part of her annual performance objectives. Project members could obtain these credits by attending the knowledge-sharing meetings set up by the PMO. In yet another case, the organization sponsored a number of employees in a master's program, through which they developed close relationships and now work at the highest levels of the organization as advocates of improved project management practice. Karen described how she and her colleagues benefited from this professional development activity:

> About two years ago, the company sponsored a master's program because they saw a need for project managers and decided, "We have to figure out some way to grow our own project managers." And so they put 10 of us through a master's program. So the 10 of us became very close in the cohort. As it turns out, one of my classmates is now the director of strategic planning.

In the summative focus group, Rachel described how she pairs junior project managers with more experienced ones who can provide mentoring on an as-needed basis:

> We set up that kind of mentoring, or however you'd want to say it. The project manager has another PM to go to (and I'm always available too), but just the idea of having another PM to go to, who you can be in the trenches with the stuff on, that could help mentor and guide through any particular process. You know, it seems to be very favorable. There's no appraisal piece to it. It's just, "Here it is. Let's talk about it," and then the PM gets to move on with it.

Reflection Throughout the Project. Reflection throughout the project, rather than only upon project closure, was identified by 10 percent of the PMO leaders as an enabler of cross-project learning. Patty described in more detail how she works with her organization to encourage reflection throughout projects rather than only at the end:

> So the two ways in which we try to achieve that, or get around that particular challenge, is we highly encourage that project team to keep a running list of lessons learned in real time, or at least conduct a formal, a more formal check-in at the end of each phase of a project. Then through our guidance and facilitation of the formal lessons learned,

we'll try to set that up in a way in which we try to kind of refresh their memories.

Similarly, in discussing his organization's lessons-learned practices, Mack mentioned that "instead of doing the lessons learned at the end, we ask teams to actually do it at the end of each phase."

Barriers to Cross-Project Learning

All the PMO leaders identified various barriers that impeded their and their organizations' efforts to learn from past project experiences. Following is a discussion of these barriers.

Lack of Direct Authority. Just over half (55 percent) of the PMO leaders in the study pointed to a lack of direct authority over project teams or project managers as making it more challenging to ensure that past learning is incorporated into new project activities. Melissa, a recently appointed PMO leader, described her reactions after attempts to begin working with a problematic project team:

> One big barrier is—"Who's Melissa coming in here? Why do we have to tell her anything? Why are we going to do what she says? She's not our manager." You know, "Who cares?" That was a huge barrier, and that's always a huge barrier, coming in as a PMO when you don't actually have these people reporting to you.

Robert, a more established PMO leader faced with similar challenges, described how he'd change things if given the authority:

> Get me out of IT. Get me into the Enterprise. Give me all the projects, all the project managers, all the initiatives, all the products, and I will save you money and will get this [stuff] done on time, on budget.

The lack of direct authority meant that for some PMO leaders, project teams were seen as working in "silos." In the cases where this occurred, the PMO leaders expressed frustration that project teams sometimes worked at "arm's length." Karen, for example, said, "You know, it's not easy to find out the details of what's going on sometimes when you're on the outside of a project." Similarly, Antonio described his relationship with project teams and how he is limited in his capacity to share or transfer lessons learned:

> A lot of these project teams sort of work in their own individual silos, if you will, and they go off and do their work. Right now the only mechanism for sharing best practices is, you know, when I'm able to communicate with them [informally]. You know, communicate to the individual project teams.

Mack demonstrated how the lack of direct authority over the project managers can lead to uncertainty about whether or not past learning is being incorporated into new projects:

> Right now there's no way for us to check if [project managers are using the lessons-learned recommendations from their knowledge-sharing forums] and have they thought about those recommendations and why they decided to do it or not to do it. So that's one issue we have.

In a striking confirmation of the frequently reported lack of direct authority, a project manager talked about how another PMO was created by one of the company's business units outside of IT, placing his PMO within IT in a precarious position:

> The biggest issue in our environment has been new PMOs that just sprung up recently, that have nothing to do with our PMO model. I think that they argue with the idea of, "What's the value of us always going to that group for expertise? I can hire the same people you guys hired. We can hire our own PMO leader, and we don't have to strive to your methodology. We can make it work for us."

Time Pressures.   Just under half of the PMO leaders (45 percent) identified some combination of time pressures and resistance on the part of organizational members to engaging in what they perceive as "extra work."

Time pressures sometimes result from project members being pulled into new projects immediately after their last project ends, making it difficult for them to take time for reflection. Sarah described how this phenomenon impedes her ability to improve future projects:

So if I were the queen of the world, then I would ask for more reflective time, time to actually decompress and—What's the word? And bring about a learning environment which is, "Yeah, just give us a little more time to get our breath before we move on to the next one," because that's how you learn the lesson. You know? Okay. Yes. The PMO can bring everybody together, and we can talk about the lessons, and I can document them, and then I can circulate them. But if that's while you're already one-third of the way into the next project, how the hell am I supposed to apply them as quickly as we're doing the projects?

Time pressures are also cited as a reason why project members may not want to take the time to follow PMO processes related to lessons learned. Darla, the PMO leader in the organization that requires documented lessons learned in order to maintain an internationally recognized quality certification, talked about the "pushback" she sometimes receives on these requirements:

They're pretty hard-core here about requiring so much documentation, so much follow-up, so many metrics. Some of them make sense for some projects and some of them don't make any sense for some projects, so I think there's a lot of pushback in getting that done. You know, when you didn't have to do it before and you suddenly do, it is a lot of extra work.

The perceived burdens of "extra process" were also highlighted by a project manager who said the following in response to the interviewer's question, "What do you think PMO leaders perceive to be their responsibilities related to the transfer of lessons learned?":

I think that their perception of a PMO is the governance, more governance, and setting the rules, setting templates, and they're almost making these templates and rules as a goal by itself. I think this is where you get, not all of it, but many of the perceptions.

People Rotating Into and Out of Roles. Just under half of the PMO leaders (45 percent) also stated that people moving into and out of project-related roles at all levels, including project managers, team members, and senior decision makers, impeded their ability to ensure that past lessons learned were consistently incorporated into new projects. Debra explained how people rotating into and out of roles confounded her efforts to ensure that past learning was brought forward:

> And that's the one thing that I'm constantly dealing with now, is the change of roles and responsibilities within the business as well as the application development area, keeping track of who's who and, "Who else do I need to bring up to speed? Who else do I need to convince? Who else do I need to have see the light?" Because that constantly changes.

Similarly, June explained the problematic impact of organizational changes and the shifting roles and responsibilities that result:

> But as a PMO, you've got people coming into and out of jobs all the time, coming from one role to another role, and are at different levels of maturity within the role that they play. If you only focus on the set-back schedules, the milestones, and the templates, you'll fail, because you have to be adaptive to the organizational constraints.

Fear of Publicly Airing Mistakes. Some of the PMO leaders (35 percent) pointed to project members' fears of publicly airing mistakes as a barrier to learning from past project experiences. Debra pointed to fears of airing mistakes publicly as a reason why she often was not invited to project teams' lessons-learned sessions:

> That's why I'm not always invited to them because it's kind of like, you know, "We don't need to air our dirty laundry." They do create the lessons learned, and they are attached (sometimes they're not). You know? So if I know a postmortem has gone on, then we'll double-check to make sure that the information has been attached. But we don't—sometimes there's sensitivity to it, so we don't need to add salt to the wound.

Similarly, Cathy talked about how project teams might not want to relate their experiences publicly because of the sensitivities involved:

> Considering lessons learned, sometimes there are folks that don't want to share that information if there was something that happened on

the project that, you know, they don't want to get out. You know? Like we had that knock-down, drag-out fight and we really don't want anybody to know about it. Not that that happened. But do you know what I mean?

Sarah talked about her experience with a project manager who she feels was afraid to speak up when problems started occurring on a project, leading to larger problems and an eventual "no-go" decision by her management team:

Unfortunately, it was because the project manager wasn't as good as she should be, and she was covering things up. You know, the price of failure was too much for her to pay, but then, you know, it caught her at the end. So every week on week, when I'd been asking, not just about me, but certainly because—we're talking about the PMO meeting. Week on week, when I was asking, "Are there any issues? Are there any resourcing constraints?" You know, whatever. It was like, "No, no. We're fine. No, we're fine."

In reaction to the finding that fear of airing mistakes was a barrier to cross-project learning, a project manager in the project manager focus group related her thoughts about this phenomenon and how it can occur in the project environment:

That's what I was going to bring up, especially when you have a string of projects that were, say, green. And then all of a sudden, you're on somewhat of a turbulent project, where it's turning red, there's a tendency to somewhat dismiss it. Because well, you don't want to kind of admit that there's something wrong. And also your manager, or whoever it may be, may tend to distance it because they had such a great experience prior to this as well. (Project Manager 3)

Reflection Deferred Until End of Project. One-fifth of the PMO leaders highlighted the problem of retrospective recall and how conducting lessons-learned sessions at the end of a project's life cycle can limit participants' ability to learn from past project experiences. Patty discussed this problem and how it can create a barrier to project members' learning from their project experiences:

Because sometimes, particularly in project teams that have been out there for a period of time, it's hard to do a formal lessons learned at the end and have them remember everything. . . . I think that if we were able to crack the nut of getting more real-time feedback of lessons learned from our teams, it would put us in a better space. I think that there's always that lag and delay of what happens to when we find it, and where we find it. It's always challenging.

Similarly, Mort described how he would change his status meeting approach so that reflection occurs more often over the course of projects:

When we're having status meetings, we should be focusing not entirely on, "Okay. Where are we against these milestones? And what issues have we raised?" We should also be asking, "What's going well?" With our success, make sure we talk about them, to understand the "whys" behind it and the "hows" where others can hear it.

Lack of Senior Management Support. One-fifth of the PMO leaders also identified a lack of senior management support as a barrier to cross-project learning. In these cases, PMO leaders stated that senior managers often do not "walk the talk" when it comes to lessons learned, and some did not even "talk the talk." For example, Melissa described the "lip service" paid to learning from the past in her organization:

Oh, the data that we get from postmortems? You know, "Gather that. And yes, we need to investigate that and make sure that doesn't happen on the next one." You know, "Check into it on the next one." So there's lip service to that. All kinds. "Absolutely that's the right thing to do." But then, when it comes down to it, "Well, that's just another task, and we don't have time for that."

In response to the question, "In what ways does the organization support your efforts to learn from project work and share those learnings with your team and other PMs?" Cathy described how the senior managers in her organization are often focused on status reporting rather than lessons learned:

You know, it's hard to say. Because that gets back to the question of, "Are they looking for the lessons learned?" And they're really not. What they are looking for is the status reporting on the projects. They're looking to share that information to know where we are, in that regard.

Organizational Members' Difficulty Accessing Past Lessons Learned. One-fifth of the PMO leaders also reported that it was difficult to share lessons learned with the right people at the right time, even if those lessons were stored in databases that were accessible via the corporate intranet. Mack talked about why he perceives databases like this to be limited in value:

> So in the past, what happened was, you know, what they do is they do gather some lessons learned and sometimes they post it in a common repository. But nobody looks at it and nobody even sees what is in those lessons learned. As I said earlier many times, documenting and just even publishing it, nobody is going to look at that.

This was echoed by a project manager in the project manager focus group, who said:

> It's more left to chance. . . . They will put lessons learned [on an intranet site], and I've seen that it even translates into revising training, as needed. But it's more than a process. It's more word of mouth. They're shared among the PMs.

The Challenges of Brokering

E. Wenger (1998) characterizes brokering as a complex process that's fraught with social challenges. As mentioned in Chapter 3, he claims that brokering requires "enough legitimacy to influence the development of a practice, mobilize attention, and address conflicting interests. It also requires the ability to link practices by facilitating transactions between them, and to cause learning by introducing into a practice elements of another" (pp. 109–110). Because boundaries lack the negotiated understanding of what defines competence in a given community of practice, the value of brokering can be difficult to recognize. As a result, "brokers sometimes interpret the uprootedness associated with brokering in personal terms of individual adequacy."

It is not surprising, then, that 55 percent of the PMO leaders reported insufficient authority over project teams as a major barrier to cross-project learning. Given their boundary-spanning role across communities, direct authority may be perceived as a route to achieving the legitimacy required in order to gain the cooperation and attention of project managers, teams, and management.

Because of the frequent mention of a lack of direct authority, additional analysis was performed to determine whether or not there was a difference in perception between those who report to "C-level" executives and those who report further down in the organizational hierarchy. It was found that approximately the same proportion of participants reporting to the C level as of those reporting elsewhere expressed a lack of direct authority, suggesting that organizational position does not necessarily make a difference in respondents' perceptions of a lack of authority affecting their ability to facilitate cross-project learning. The researcher posits that it is not necessarily organizational position that creates the required level of authority, but the perceived legitimacy of the PMO leader, regardless of where he reports.

According to Wenger, brokering requires the ability to "manage carefully the coexistence of membership and non-membership, yielding enough distance to bring a different perspective, but also enough legitimacy to be listened to" (p. 110). The two most frequently expressed enablers of cross-project learning—a strong network of good relationships and support from senior management—can be seen as both contributors to and by-products of the level of legitimacy required of the PMO leader if he is to mobilize the activities required to facilitate learning from one project to the next.

As discussed in Chapter 3, Cervero and Wilson (2001) claim that adult learning in any context represents a struggle for knowledge and power. Learning not only is shaped by relations of power, but plays a role in reproducing or changing these relations. Taking this perspective, the negotiation of meaning associated with project lessons learned can also be seen as a political endeavor, the results of which depend on the relative power associated with project teams, management, and the PMO.

Project teams can exercise power by excluding the PMO from discussions of project lessons learned. Likewise, the PMO leader can exercise power by intervening with project teams to facilitate learning. The learning that results in either case will necessarily be negotiated based on the interests of those involved and may give certain interests priority over others. For example, if the PMO leader is involved and has garnered sufficient legitimacy, the learning outcomes may be shaped by the PMO leader's interest in the project team's conformance to existing standards and processes. Did they follow established routines? Why or why not? In situations where the PMO leader is not present or has not attained a sufficient level of legitimacy, emphasis may be placed elsewhere, as the project team may not have a vested interest in improving the organization's project standards and processes.

Social Capital. A strong network and support from senior management are closely aligned with the concept of social capital, which J. Nahapiet and S. Ghoshal (1998) define as "the sum of the actual and potential resources embedded within, available through, and derived from, the network of relationships possessed by an individual or social unit"(p. 243). It appears that the social capital of the PMO leader is an important factor in her ability to gain the legitimacy required to facilitate cross-project learning, particularly when she lacks a direct line of authority over project participants.

Defensive Routines. Insufficient authority was not the only challenge reported by PMO leaders. As shown earlier in the chapter, 45 percent of interviewees also reported time pressures as a barrier to learning from past project experiences. One might simply surmise that if organizational members do not have the time to engage in learning practices, then processes associated with replicating success and avoiding past failures may simply require increased visibility and attention in order to be effectively deployed. Yet this conclusion may not tell the whole story, especially given that, as reported earlier, 50 percent of the PMO leaders indicate that upper management expects them to continuously improve project delivery.

Researchers in previous project-based learning studies have also noted time pressures as a barrier to learning from past project experiences (Disterer, 2002; Keegan & Turner, 2001; Schindler & Eppler, 2003; Zedtwitz, 2003). In A. Keegan and J. R. Turner's study of 19 project-based firms, for example, the authors found that it was "common throughout the study for respondents to list impressive practices in place to facilitate organizational learning, and then at the very end to state they do not work, or are not used, because of the time pressures on those people whose learning is the focus of these systems" (p. 91).

It may not be simply a lack of time that limits the use of reflective practices, but rather defensive routines that conspire to make conscious reflection and learning much less appealing to organizational members than, say, launching the next project and generating more activity. As described in earlier chapters, Chris Argyris (1995) describes organizational defensive routines as "any action, policy, or practice that prevents organizational participants from experiencing embarrassment or threat and, at the same time, prevents them from discovering the causes of the embarrassment or threat" (pp. 20–22). "Face-saving" is one such defensive routine, the rules of which Argyris describes as follows: "When encountering embarrassment or threat, bypass it and cover up the bypass."

It is not difficult to envision defensive routines at work within the project environment, especially within the context of red-light learning, where management and the PMO intervene with project teams to understand what went wrong after a project has been classified as red on the PMO leader's dashboard status report. One could also envision defensive routines at work not only at the project team level, but also at the PMO leader level and among members of the management team. Each of these communities, either by its action or by its inaction, may have the potential to be seen as a contributor to "the problem." Of course, project team members—and especially project managers—are under a more acute threat to their individual careers. The point here is that the PMO leader and the senior management team, because of their relative positions of power, can inadvertently undermine their own ability to "know the truth" about what is happening at the project level. After all, defensive routines are likely to emerge if project members have the potential to be associated with a "mistake."

In sum, then, under conditions of red-light learning, reflective practices can come to be seen by the culture as a punitive experience, making it more likely that defensive routines will be perpetuated and further reducing the utility and effectiveness of reflective practices. Defensive routines are likely to undermine the PMO leader's attempts to help team members

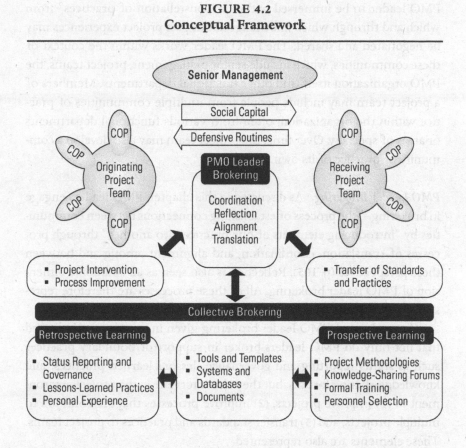

FIGURE 4.2
Conceptual Framework

reflect constructively on past project experiences for the benefit of current or future projects.

Conceptual Framework for the PMO Leader Role

A conceptual framework for how PMO leaders broker the continuous improvement process is presented in Figure 4.2. It synthesizes the findings and discussion in this chapter and includes the following elements: organizational context, PMO leader brokering, social capital, defensive routines, and collective brokering. Each of these elements is discussed here.

Organizational Context. Consistent with Wenger's (1998) view that organizations are made up of multiple communities of practice, we find the

PMO leader to be immersed within a "constellation of practices" from which and through which knowledge about past project experiences may be negotiated and shared. The PMO leader works within the context of these communities, which include senior management, project teams, the PMO organization itself, and other functional departments. Members of a project team may include people from multiple communities of practice within the organization, often from various functional departments or areas of specialty. Over time, the project team may also develop a community of practice of its own.

PMO Leader Brokering. As discussed in this chapter, PMO leaders engage in brokering—the process of establishing connections between communities by "introducing elements of one practice into another" through processes of translation, coordination, and alignment among and between these perspectives (p. 105). Reflection is also seen as an additional dimension of PMO leader brokering. All of these processes are therefore represented in the revised conceptual framework.

The analysis of PMO leader brokering given in this chapter indicated that not only do PMO leaders broker in support of boundary practices such as status reporting and governance, lessons-learned practices, and knowledge-sharing forums, but they also intervene in the project environment to (1) improve projects, (2) improve processes that are common to multiple projects, and (3) transfer standards and practices to project teams. These elements are also represented.

Social Capital and Defensive Routines. Two broad themes emerged from the additional interpretation of the enablers and barriers to cross-project learning. Social capital is seen as being a key enabler, while defensive routines are viewed as a key barrier. Researchers in project-based learning have drawn upon the concept of social capital to describe how knowledge, particularly context-dependent, tacit knowledge, is more effectively shared and diffused across projects and organizations by individuals who have developed strong, mutually beneficial relationships and have therefore gained a degree of social capital (Bresnen et al., 2003; DeFillippi & Arthur, 1998; Newell, 2004; Walker & Christenson, 2005).

As discussed previously in this chapter, red-light learning and the associated defensive routines it inspires may contribute to Keegan and Turner's (2001) finding that "in no single company did respondents express satisfaction with [the lessons-learned process]" (p. 90). Both social capital and defensive routines are represented in the revised conceptual framework.

Retrospective and Prospective Collective Learning Practices. Many of the PMO leader's activities can be classified as either retrospective, prospective, or both. Retrospective learning practices include status reporting and governance, lessons-learned practices, and the personal experiences of PMO leaders and their staffs. Prospective learning practices include project methodologies, knowledge-sharing forums, formal training, and personnel selection.

Boundary practices such as status reporting and governance, lessons-learned practices, project methodologies, and knowledge-sharing forums—all forms of collective brokering—are viewed as organizational routines (Bresnen et al., 2005) through which and by which knowledge is captured and transferred for the benefit of current and future projects. M. Bresnen et al. (2005) describe organizational routines as "repetitive, recognizable patterns of interdependent actions involving multiple actors" (p. 28). The development of these routines represents a shared history of learning (Wenger, 1998) among management, the PMO, and project teams. Collective brokering practices are a means through which lessons learned are transferred from one project to another. Newly established project managers and project teams experience these practices, with previous lessons built in, as a form of legitimate peripheral participation (Lave & Wenger, 1991).

Boundary practices can also be construed as a means by which process knowledge from past project experiences can be embedded into organizational routines for the benefit of future projects. S. Newell et al. (2006) describe process knowledge as processes that a team has deployed in order to achieve its goals. Process knowledge can be distinguished from "product knowledge," which the authors define as "knowledge about what had actually been achieved in relation to the stated goals or objectives" of a project (p. 175). The transfer of project methodologies, including embedded process knowledge, is accomplished through templates that are often stored on intranet portals for use across multiple projects. Templates and systems are forms of boundary objects that facilitate knowledge transfer through processes involving participation and reification (Wenger, 1998). Consistent with the findings of Marc Antoni et al. (2005), process knowledge resides in templates, checklists, manuals, and guidelines, representing an accumulation of experience in project delivery.

Drawing on the work of Maurizio Zollo and Sidney Winter (2002) and Martha Feldman and Brian Pentland (2003), Bresnen et al. (2005) claim that organizational learning "concerns how change is accomplished through the development of capabilities tied to the production and reproduction of new organizational routines" (p. 29). Adopting this perspective, PMO leaders can therefore be viewed as knowledge brokers who, through the establishment of both retrospective and prospective collective brokering processes, help their organizations learn from past project experiences by embedding process knowledge into organizational routines that can be transferred to new or existing projects.

The revised conceptual framework informs the cross-project and organizational learning literature in two ways. First, previous researchers have pointed to the potentially broader applicability of process knowledge than of product knowledge, suggesting that it may be a more useful mechanism by which to transfer knowledge from one project to the next (Antoni et al., 2005; Newell et al., 2006). This study confirms that process knowledge can indeed be useful in the project environment, as it demonstrates how PMO leaders utilize process knowledge in the form of project methodologies, tools, and templates to inform the work of prospective project teams.

A second way in which the revised conceptual framework informs the literature is by demonstrating that PMOs can be viewed as a way to facilitate organizational learning in project environments. As discussed in Chapter 1, Marsick and Watkins (1999) claim that organizational learning can occur if two criteria are satisfied: (1) Individuals, either appointed by management or anointed by followers, "take their learning back to the system," and (2) the system has "structures, processes and a culture in place to embed and support organizational learning" (p. 12). This study demonstrates that PMO leaders can in fact bring learning "back to the system" and that they routinely establish processes, structures, and systems that embed this learning across project teams within their organizations.

THE PMO AND MULTI-LEVEL LEARNING

A number of conclusions can be drawn about the role of the PMO leader and how he can contribute to facilitating cross-project learning and continuous improvement, components of multi-level learning that enable continuous systems-level learning. Each of these conclusions is discussed here, followed by recommendations for how PMO leaders can overcome many of the barriers to continuous improvement.

The PMO Leader as Knowledge Broker

The first conclusion drawn from the study is that PMO leaders are knowledge brokers who facilitate connections among multiple communities in order to facilitate learning from one project to the next. PMO leaders are uniquely positioned to facilitate the deployment of reflective practices and to embed this learning into future project activities for two reasons. First, by virtue of their organizational position, PMO leaders are able to see patterns across multiple projects and identify learning opportunities based on those observations. Second, PMO leaders oversee the design and implementation of processes that are common to multiple projects, and, as seen in this study, most of these practitioners have recognized the importance of embedding lessons-learned practices into project methodologies within their organization.

Transferring Improved Practices via Organizational Routines

The second conclusion is that organizational routines that can be utilized by multiple projects can provide project organizations with a repeatable way to generate and transfer learning from past project experiences. Previous theorists and researchers have identified organizational routines as a means by which the collective know-how from previous experiences can be embedded into the everyday work of organizational members (M. C. Becker, 2005; M. C. Becker et al., 2005; Bresnen et al., 2005; Feldman & Pentland, 2003; Szulanski & Jensen, 2004). As discussed in Chapter 1, however, project organizations present a unique challenge for organizational learning because projects may be perceived as being "one-off" or unique. Moreover, project teams disband upon the completion of their work, leaving no formal corpus behind to carry the learning to future activities. This study demonstrates that organizational routines in the project management environment can help to overcome these challenges. Not only do they provide a formal mechanism for lessons-learned practices, but they can incorporate learning from past project experiences in the form of improved project methodologies and templates that can be transferred to future project teams.

Legitimacy and the Need for Social Capital

The third conclusion drawn from this study is that both the learning process and the transfer of learning via organizational routines are shaped by relations of power, requiring PMO leaders to attain a degree of social capital in order to facilitate cross-project learning effectively. Project managers and teams must factor in the interests of the PMO and the processes that it requires when planning approaches to new projects. Likewise, the PMO leader must factor in the interests of project managers and teams when designing new or improved routines to ensure that they can be adopted effectively. When the PMO leader faces challenges to her legitimacy, both the learning process and the transfer of learning via organizational routines can be undermined by the relative power of project teams and senior management, both of which may be more worried about effective outcomes than about the processes by which these outcomes are achieved.

Defensive Routines Undermine Improvement

The fourth conclusion from this study is that defensive routines may distort or constrain organizational learning from projects, making it less likely that future project teams will benefit from the experiences of previous teams. Under conditions of red-light learning, where the organization focuses most of its formal reflective practices on failing projects, project team members may be inclined to avoid embarrassment or threat and may find ways to divert attention to other, less threatening issues. As a result, the learning that occurred at the individual or group level may not be adequately represented, making it more likely that future project teams will be required to "reinvent the wheel."

Lack of Awareness of the Importance of Productive Reflection

The fifth and final conclusion that can be drawn from this study is that although most PMO leaders engage in reflective practices, they may not be aware of the value of these practices when it comes to facilitating organizational learning from one project to the next. As discussed in Chapter 5, most PMO leaders engage in reflective practices in order to bring "runaway" projects back into alignment with management expectations. It may be that reflective practices are utilized more as a short-term "fix" than as a way to make a project team's tacit knowledge explicit for the benefit of future project teams.

RECOMMENDATIONS FOR PMO LEADERS

Several recommendations are provided for PMO leaders who are endeavoring to improve their organization's ability to learn from past project experiences. Overall, these recommendations are aimed at establishing conditions in which organizational members can reflect productively on past experiences by increasing the social capital of the PMO leader and reducing the effects of defensive routines.

Recommendation 1: *Focus on Accumulating Social Capital Across Multiple Communities by Establishing a Network of Strong Relationships Built on Trust, Professional Development, and Mutual Understanding.* As knowledge brokers among multiple communities of practice, PMO leaders must maintain enough distance from each community to be able to offer balanced perspectives, yet they also need to attain a degree of legitimacy among these communities in order to mobilize attention. This is true even for those who report to the highest levels of management (C-level direct reports), as formal authority does not always equate to perceived legitimacy among constituents. Therefore, it is essential that PMO leaders build a strong network across communities in order to enlist support and negotiate practice connections effectively. Given the likely pervasiveness of defensive routines and their confounding effects on reflection and learning, it is necessary to gain the trust of organizational members by emphasizing professional development over more punitive approaches and by understanding the needs of each community and its members rather than imposing practices that demonstrate a lack of understanding of a community's unique requirements.

Recommendation 2: *Focus Equal Emphasis on Learning from Successful Projects as from Those That Appear to Have Failed or Run Off Course.* If formal learning practices are continually focused on poorly performing projects, the organization risks enculturating learning practices as a punitive endeavor, making engaging in this process a less-than-appealing prospect for organizational members. Moreover, if learning practices are primarily focused on troubled projects, then the improvements in organizational routines that result may be distorted in the direction of eliminating risk and establishing tighter controls to prevent such problems from recurring. This may shackle future project teams with burdensome processes that limit their innovative potential. It is recommended that PMO leaders actively engage successful project teams in formal learning practices by adopting the multi-level learning practices described in this book, not only to make the learning process more effective and engaging, but to discover the reasons why projects succeed so that this knowledge can also be embedded in future project routines.

Recommendation 3: *Reflect over the Course of Projects Rather than Just at the End.* Performing lessons-learned sessions upon project completion is often ineffective when learning and reflection have not been part of the project from the beginning. Project teams may not have recorded their learning as the project progressed, nor will they have learned to reflect collectively in a structured format, and these limitations can severely hinder their ability to do so once at the end and expect a productive result. For projects that last for months or years, project members will clearly have difficulties bringing to the surface memories about the ways in which they solved problems over the course of the project, making the learning generated in lessons-learned sessions highly selective and potentially less than useful for future teams. It is recommended that PMO leaders adopt multi-level learning practices that embed formal reflective processes throughout the course of projects.

Recommendation 4: *Provide Useful Process Knowledge to Project Teams by Asking "Why" Questions in Lessons-Learned Sessions and Embedding Stories and Examples from Past Project Experiences into Standard Methodologies and Templates.*   Most of the lessons-learned practices described by PMO leaders focused on "what worked and what didn't" with respect to past project activities. It is recommended that these reflective questions be supplemented with questions as to *why* something worked or did not. This may generate more useful knowledge not only for the project team that is reflecting on the experiences, but for prospective project teams that need to heed this advice on future projects. Asking why can evoke richer contextual information about why the practice worked or did not so that future project teams can make informed choices about their planned approaches. This richer contextual information may also be accompanied by what was formerly tacit knowledge on the part of the originating project team, making this knowledge more accessible to the organization.

Recommendation 5: *Establish Conditions That Are More Conducive to Productive Reflection in Lessons-Learned Sessions by Utilizing an Objective, Substantively Neutral Facilitator.*   Lessons-learned sessions can be dominated by defensive routines, which can distort the reflective process and block learning at the project level. The "lessons" that result may therefore not represent the true experiences of project teams, further undermining the organization's ability to continuously improve. It is recommended that PMO leaders provide a means for project teams to utilize a trained facilitator from outside the project team who can help the team uncover its tacit knowledge and provide conditions that foster equal participation so that organizational members' defensive routines do not dominate the session. A skilled facilitator from outside the team can help the group members avoid "blamestorming" and focus on the processes by which they achieved their outcomes rather than focusing on the performance of specific individuals, thus creating an atmosphere that is less conducive to defensiveness, blame, or individual heroics.

CONCLUSION

This chapter presented the findings from interviews with 20 PMO leaders and two focus groups. It described how the PMO leader plays a critical knowledge brokering role, working across communities of practice to facilitate continuous improvement. As the overseer of multiple concurrent projects, the PMO is able to incorporate learning practices and the outcomes that result into the organization's routines, methodologies, systems, tools, and templates. It is in this way that the PMO leader provides the "glue" that enables continuous systems-level learning.

PART 3

Implementing Multi-Level Learning

In Part 2, we discussed two of the roles required for deploying multi-level learning: the multi-level learning coach and the program management office (PMO). In this section, we discuss how the people in these roles work with the rest of the organization to facilitate learning and continuous innovation at each of three levels: projects, processes, and strategies. The first chapter covers how to facilitate continuous innovation and improvement at the project team level. The second chapter discusses how to engage project managers and teams in improving processes that span multiple projects. The third chapter in Part 3 focuses on how to facilitate alignment between the organization's strategy and its overall project portfolio.

5 | FACILITATING LEVEL 1: CONTINUOUS PROJECT IMPROVEMENT

Level 1, facilitating continuous project improvement, focuses on providing mechanisms that allow project teams to learn from their experience while work is progressing. In Chapter 1, we discussed the need for continuous structured learning throughout the project life cycle, so that teams can generate actions based on their reflective efforts while something can still be done to improve their results. Among the numerous problems with postproject reviews is that team members lack the motivation to tackle sensitive or complex issues head-on after the project is over, since addressing these issues can no longer improve the outcomes. Continuous structured learning over the course of projects enables teams to reflect and improve while they are "in flight," reducing the risk of the surprises and blowups that can result when problems remain buried or unresolved.

OVERVIEW OF LEVEL 1: CONTINUOUS PROJECT IMPROVEMENT

Consistent with the principles of multi-level learning discussed in Chapter 2, the purpose of Level 1, continuous project improvement, is to give project teams a mechanism for reflecting on their experiences in order to eliminate waste, deliver as fast as possible, and satisfy the customer while seeing the whole and welcoming new insights as they emerge. They do this by taking responsibility for their own learning, using a third-party coach to facilitate action-reflection cycles at key points in the project, either after each iteration or upon the completion of key milestones.

After each iteration or phase, the project team assembles to look back on what results were actually delivered and to what extent the team has met the expectations for that time period. The project retrospective is different from a standard project review. It is not meant to replace it. Standard project reviews are informational. They provide the senior team or the PMO with updates on what a project has delivered, its status, and what needs to happen next to either get it back on track or keep it running. The focus is on the project team receiving feedback from the key decision makers, emphasizing what the team should be doing to meet expectations. The project retrospective is different. Consistent with the principle of empowering teams to take responsibility for their own learning, it asks the team members to reflect on what actions they need to take to continually improve on their results. The project retrospective enables team members to reflect on the project without the added complexity of "saving face" or defending their approach in the presence of their peers or managers.

As noted in Chapter 3, the multi-level learning coach has no decision-making authority and serves as a substantively neutral third party. She works with the team's project manager to plan and conduct prospective and retrospective sessions to clarify what needs to be done, reflect on what was actually accomplished, and plan improvements for the next time period. While the PMO leader or his designate may or may not attend these sessions, a key function of the PMO is to capture the learning and knowledge that results so that they can be applied to other projects and programs that can use them.

The project manager takes the lead role in prospective discussions, with facilitation support from the coach, while the coach takes the lead in facilitating the retrospective.

We now turn to the steps required at this level. As shown in Figure 5.1, these include (1) plan and conduct the prospective, (2) execute the plan, (3) plan and conduct the retrospective, and (4) update project plans, issues, risks, and lessons learned. Coverage of each of these steps follows, beginning with Step 1.

FIGURE 5.1
Steps for Level 1: Continuous Project Improvement

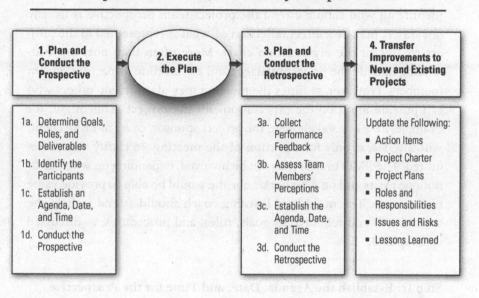

STEP 1: PLAN AND CONDUCT THE PROSPECTIVE

Before conducting the first prospective with the project team, the coach works with the project manager to (a) determine the goals, roles, and deliverables for the next iteration or time period, (b) identify the participants, (c) establish the agenda, date, and time, and (d) conduct the prospective.

Step 1a: Determine the Goals, Roles, and Deliverables

The primary purpose of the prospective is to confirm and clarify the goals, roles, and deliverables for the next time period or iteration. As this becomes more routine, teams will be able to get into a "flow" where they plan, execute, and reflect at regular intervals. The project manager (or the Scrum master for agile teams) confirms their understanding of the objectives and deliverables in preparation for the session, getting input from team members, sponsors, and business owners as required.

Step 1b: Identify the Participants

Identifying who should attend the project team prospective is usually obvious. It may be a direct reflection of what is represented in the project charter or the organization chart. More often than not, those attending include the project manager and all full-time or part-time team members. However, at times the meeting may also include others who can provide input on the expectations for the project. This might, for example, be a key stakeholder, the project sponsor, or an internal client, who attends, if only for a portion of the meeting, to clarify what is required. The PMO may or may not be involved, depending on whether or not one exists and on whether or not she would be able to provide value to the team. The multi-level learning coach should attend to help the team clarify and reinforce its goals, roles, and procedures, as discussed in Chapter 3.

Step 1c: Establish the Agenda, Date, and Time for the Prospective

Each prospective may have a different emphasis, depending on what stage in its life cycle the strategy or program is in and how much experience the team has with these types of sessions. Yet regardless of where the project or the team members are in relation to progress or experience, the purpose of the prospective is to come to agreement on the answers to the following questions for the upcoming period, phase, or iteration. These questions serve as the outline of the agenda:

1. What are the objectives and deliverables expected to be completed by the team?
2. What are the roles and responsibilities of each individual with respect to making this happen?
3. What are the time and budget constraints?

The project manager will need to use his judgment, based on the preliminary conversations and preparations, as to how much time should be dedicated to each of these areas. In all cases, before addressing these topics in sequential fashion, the project manager, with assistance from the coach, facilitates a discussion about the ground rules for group discussions (see

Chapter 3) and ensures that time is allocated to this task on the agenda, particularly for the first prospective.

Step 1d: Conduct the Prospective

Unlike the retrospective, which may place people in a defensive posture and therefore needs to be facilitated by the multi-level learning coach, the prospective may be led by the project manager or Scrum master (in the case of agile projects), provided that she is skilled in the use of effective group intervention and the principles of multi-level learning described in Chapters 2 and 3, respectively. The coach may intervene when required to keep the group on track, while the project manager leads the team in getting clarity on objectives, deliverables, and time and budget constraints. Doing so sets the stage for the group members to take action in the next iteration or phase, knowing that in a few weeks' time they will reflect as a group on what worked, what didn't, and what they need to sustain or change the next time around. Participants are asked to keep a journal of their experiences so that they can bring this material to the retrospective session.

STEP 2: EXECUTE THE PLAN

After having clarified the goals, roles, and deliverables, the project manager, in consultation with the team members, issues a project plan that outlines who will do what, and when. The team then goes to work to carry out that plan, working to meet the goals and deliverables defined in the prospective. As work proceeds, the team members may wish to record significant events in individual journals and reflect on them as they occur. This will provide more useful material for discussions during the retrospective, which follows next.

STEP 3: PLAN AND CONDUCT THE RETROSPECTIVE

After each iteration, every 30 days, or after significant milestones, the project team reassembles to look back on what results were actually delivered and to what extent the team has met the expectations for that time period. In this step, the coach works with the project manager to lay the groundwork for the session. Unlike the prospective, however, this session is facilitated by the coach. In this step, the project manager and coach work together to (a) collect performance feedback, (b) assess team members' perceptions, (c) establish the agenda, date, and time, and (d) conduct the retrospective.

Step 3a: Collect Performance Feedback

As discussed in Chapter 2, the principles of multi-level learning encourage quick iterations of project delivery that place working end products in users' hands sooner, so that teams can get feedback, learn, improve, and deliver what customers actually need and want. Measures of on-time performance and budget variances are useful as intermediary measures and provide information that may be useful in reflecting on recent events. However, short iterations that give customers and internal clients the ability to offer their perceptions are much more effective. Regular feedback from customers early in the cycle can reduce waste and focus resources on the right areas sooner. Of course, short iterations are an ideal, and they are not always possible for all types of projects.

For organizations that provide project services directly to external customers, assessing customer satisfaction may be more straightforward, albeit not always easy. Many project organizations, however, provide project services to internal clients. For example, IT may develop new software and systems for the call center, or a Six Sigma group may perform projects that help the HR group. The HR group, in turn, may perform projects for the operations group. Distinguishing between external customers and internal clients is consistent with one of the core principles of multi-level learning: Satisfy the customer. In all cases, and wherever feasible and possible, providing value to the external customer is the ultimate goal. In the case of projects that deliver to internal clients, however, assessing the internal client's satisfaction while keeping the external customer in mind may be the most pragmatic approach.

In addition to gathering internal client or external customer feedback wherever possible, it is also beneficial to obtain perceptual, qualitative feedback from the project's sponsors and other senior managers.

Questions for these stakeholders might include: What topics should the team address in the retrospective? What are some of the strengths of the work to date? In which areas should the team focus its improvement efforts? It is important to emphasize that stakeholders' perceptions may not reflect the deep level of understanding that the project team has developed as a result of having been close to the details of the work. Feedback from sponsors and stakeholders, therefore, should be understood as perceptual data. Yet this feedback provides the team members with important information that will help them better understand what is on the minds of the people who may have significant impact on the project in one way or another.

It is also useful to have factual data related to actual person-hours, actual output (lines of code, for example), and the number of defects, delays, and schedule slips. Having these data will help in establishing a fact base that enables the team to see the amount of work accomplished, to improve future time and resource estimates, and to identify areas that can be improved upon. Examples of the questions for data collection might include the following:

1. What were the calendar time and number of person-hours required at each stage?
2. What were the schedule slips on the project, if any, and when did they occur?
3. How many defects were found at each stage, and how did these defects affect the project or its key stakeholders?
4. What are the customer, internal client, or sponsor's perceptions regarding the project's progress?

Step 3b: Assess Team Members' Perceptions

Prior to the session, particularly for end-of-project retrospectives or for those that occur after significant milestones, the coach will need to speak individually with each team member to do the following:

1. Describe the retrospective process and its benefits (for those who are new to the process).
2. Ask the team member what topics he feels need to be addressed.

3. Ask him to describe what he feels would make for a successful retrospective result.
4. Determine if there are areas of particular sensitivity that need to be handled with care.
5. Ask him to collect artifacts, including his project calendar, personal diaries, memos, meeting notes, old project schedules, white papers, budgets, project plans, project resource allocation, personnel "loading" charts, and any other materials that may be useful. These materials may be found in the team member's journals, old e-mails, notebooks, bug status reports, MS Project files, and so on, and should be brought to the meeting.

These conversations, particularly for the first senior team retrospective, enable the coach to build rapport, prepare an agenda, and identify potential "hot buttons" that may lead to defensive routines. They also provide an opportunity to talk about what each member needs to bring to the session in the form of artifacts. These may be drawn from the team members' individual journals, e-mail exchanges, meeting notes, presentations, or project reviews and will be shared by each member during the retrospective. They serve as a means for communicating agreement and focusing on actual events, so that each member of the group is able to provide perspective on the things that he feels are most important for discussion. This helps to both refresh memories and keep the focus on actual facts and events.

Step 3c: Establish the Agenda, Date, and Time

As discussed in Chapter 2, the purpose of the retrospective is to reflect on the actual results so that the team can plan actions that will improve future performance and build on its successes. The agenda for the project retrospective should result in answers to the following questions:

1. What were our expectations, objectives, and deliverables for this time period?
2. What were the actual results that were delivered? What were the perceptions of internal clients, customers, and other key stakeholders with regard to these outcomes?

3. What were the primary causes or determinants of these results and perceptions, whether favorable or unfavorable?
4. What worked well that we don't want to forget?
5. What should we do differently next time?

The coach will design her agenda to achieve these objectives based on the planning discussions and her style preferences for how to accomplish them. As with the prospective, the meeting should start by establishing or reviewing ground rules for group interaction, including Kerth's Prime Directive (see Chapter 3 for a more detailed discussion of this). In addition, the following agenda items should also be included:

1. *Review expectations, objectives, and deliverables.* This should be brief and to the point.
2. *Discuss what actually occurred with respect to these areas.* Record team members' perceptions on a flip chart, ensuring that you get clarity concerning what's being said.
3. *Share artifacts.* In the planning discussions, group members were asked to bring important artifacts to the session, including their journals, project calendars, schedules, resource allocations, requirements, and the like. Allocate time for each person to discuss the artifacts he brought. Particularly for end-of-project retrospectives, N. Kerth (2001) suggests that the team vote and award prizes to the people who bring the most artifacts, the most significant artifact, and the most unusual artifact. This brings a degree of levity and humor that can be very effective, as long as the organization's culture is supportive of this kind of activity.
4. *Develop a timeline.* Before the session, hang blank flip charts on the wall and title them with applicable time buckets from left to right in chronological order. Have large Post-it notes available for individuals to record specific events. Facilitate the development of a timeline of important events that occurred over the course of the previous time period. This can be done either by asking the group to break out into small groups or take a few minutes for each individual to record her events on a series of Post-it notes. The approach chosen will depend on the size of the group and the ability of specific group members to collaborate effectively. Begin with the start of the project or time period, and ask each person or subgroup to offer its Post-it notes. Put

them on the flip charts under the applicable time period, reading each aloud as you post it, and clarifying the event if necessary so that all team members understand the message that is being conveyed.

5. *Offer appreciations.* This is an exercise developed by Kerth (2001) that can be used to help team members appreciate all the work they've accomplished, particularly if they perceive the project to be less than successful. The facilitator asks the group for a volunteer who would like to express appreciation for someone else's efforts. The person who receives the appreciation then selects someone whom she would like to thank, and the cycle continues until all individuals have both given and received appreciations. The coach will need to decide whether or not a group is ready for such an activity and whether or not it will be helpful. You will find, however, that many teams will respond to this activity favorably, as this kind of opportunity is a rare event in the everyday work experience!

6. *Identify what caused the results, whether favorable or unfavorable.* This is a critically important part of the session that is often neglected in postproject reviews. Working from the timeline and their collective memory, the team members should attempt to come to a common understanding of what led to the results, whether these results were perceived as positive or negative. It may be useful for the facilitator to introduce the concept of the "five whys," an exercise that is familiar to those with knowledge of quality improvement tools. Often, the root causes of specific outcomes lie buried within statements of fact and require additional answers to the question "why" in order to be uncovered. For example, if the project was delayed by two weeks, the facilitator begins by asking "why." A response might be, "Because the requirements were not clear." The facilitator then asks "why" once again. A response might be, "Because we didn't talk to the right people to get the requirements." The sequence then continues until either five whys have been asked or a suitable cause has been identified. This can be a tricky exercise for a variety of reasons. First, it is absolutely critical to ensure that people do not blame specific individuals or groups, but rather take collective responsibility for the result. It should be assumed that each person did the best he could at the time, so the focus of the cause analysis should be on decisions, issues, procedures, and processes associated with the group as a whole rather than perceptions about

problems with specific individuals. The aim is to create an environment of safety so that the group can have a genuinely productive discussion. Second, this exercise can be tricky because what constitutes a "root cause" is not always obvious or unequivocal. The best approach is to be pragmatic and use the following criterion: A root cause is something that, if it were eliminated or adequately addressed, would prevent the same problem from recurring. Note that it is possible to identify the root causes of successful results as well.

7. *Identify solutions for overcoming problems and replicating successes.* Facilitate the brainstorming of solutions that, if applied the next time, could prevent problems from recurring or enable successes to be carried forward. These solutions should be based on the causes of the actual outcomes discussed in the previous step, consistent with the problem-solving model reviewed in Chapter 3.

8. *Identify action items.* Questions to ask here include the following:
   a. What worked well that we don't want to forget?
   b. What should we do differently next time?
   c. What requires more data, expertise, or discussion to better understand?

Norm Kerth (2001), Esther Derby and Diana Larsen (2006) provide a number of additional tools that can be used for retrospectives with project teams, including (for those familiar with quality tools) brainstorming, force field analysis, and fishbone, all of which can be useful depending on the situation at hand.

Step 3d: Conduct the Retrospective

Unlike the prospective, which may be facilitated by the project manager or Scrum master, the retrospective is facilitated by the coach—an objective third party with no influence over performance reviews and no decision-making authority on a day-to-day basis. As a skilled facilitator of learning and reflection, she helps team members look back on the project work in ways that limit defensive routines, reminding people about tools such as TALK, the Ladder of Inference, and collaborative conflict resolution that emphasizes understanding of underlying needs rather than bargaining positions (see Chapter 3 for a detailed discussion of how and under what circumstances the coach should intervene to keep the group on track). When retrospectives are conducted more frequently, the team members themselves will become skilled in the art of asking questions that lead to valid information, free and informed choice, and internal commitment.

STEP 4: UPDATE PROJECT PLANS, ISSUES, RISKS, AND LESSONS LEARNED

After the retrospective session, the project manager or Scrum leader works with the coach and the PMO leader to document the results and communicate them to team members, sponsors, and key stakeholders. "Report-out" meetings with senior managers and the PMO may be useful for generating support for the team's improvement actions. In addition, subgroups of individuals may be required to take certain actions as a result of the meeting and to make adjustments to the project charter, the project plan, and the issues and risks logs that are often maintained by project and program teams. Updates to the following documents may be required to ensure that the improvements are taken into the next iteration or time period:

- Action items
- The project charter (including objectives, scope, and business case)
- The project plan and resource allocations
- Roles and responsibilities
- Issue and risk logs
- Other "learning" that the team wants captured in the form of things to sustain or improve

The project manager or Scrum master works with the PMO leader or program manager to follow up on important improvements that need to be carried forward, including the decisions captured in the documents just listed. What matters most is that the team acts on the outcomes of the retrospective and that its members find the experience valuable. Therefore, it is good practice for the coach to facilitate feedback on the retrospective process itself, modeling the behavior of taking feedback and acting upon it as appropriate so that the team feels that it is being listened to and that it has an adequate degree of control over its group process and how it is spending its time.

CONCLUSION

Project team retrospectives at regular intervals in the project life cycle enable teams to reflect, learn, and improve as they go. With the help of the multi-level learning coach, they take responsibility for their own learning so that they can proactively address problems, issues, and risks wherever possible before they grow into surprises or blowups that trigger a red light. Of course, problems will always arise unexpectedly, but when teams have honed their communication skills and reflective capacity through frequent action-reflection cycles, they are able to solve these problems more effectively as they occur, rather than waiting until the end of the project, when the damage has already been done. Regular feedback from customers through short iterations, although not always possible, provides the opportunity to focus on only those areas that are important to the customer, enabling the team to reduce waste and deliver only what customers truly require.

In the next chapter, we cover how to facilitate cross-project improvements that enable innovations to be spread from one team to the next, creating a multiplier effect that has the potential to improve results across many projects in the portfolio simultaneously.

6 | FACILITATING LEVEL 2: CROSS-PROJECT IMPROVEMENT

Many project organizations are small in scale, with one or two teams at most working on projects at the same time. For these organizations, the people who develop improvements are not different from the ones who use them in the next project. In larger project organizations, however, and on business transformation initiatives that require many concurrent work streams, there may be numerous or even hundreds of projects going at the same time. People who work in these environments know that while each project is unique—having its own set of objectives, plans, issues, and risks—many of them follow common steps. In these situations, one team may benefit from improvements and innovations made by another. At this level of multi-level learning, knowledge and innovation are shared across projects to improve processes that are common to multiple projects. This creates a "multiplier effect," in which improvements can not only improve team efficiency and effectiveness, but enable the organization as a whole to continuously improve, reduce waste, and deliver faster across many projects at the same time.

This chapter covers how to apply the principles of multi-level learning to facilitate cross-project improvement. It begins with an overview of this level and then moves to a discussion of the steps required to make it happen.

OVERVIEW OF LEVEL 2: CROSS-PROJECT IMPROVEMENT

The goal of Level 2 is to provide a mechanism for continually improving performance across multiple projects. Cross-project improvement is different from Six Sigma or other process improvement methodologies that use a "waterfall" approach. Rather than following a sequential project plan that steps through the phases of define, measure, analyze, and improve, cross-project improvement is an iterative approach. It starts with data from project-level retrospectives and an improvement goal. Project managers then try new approaches on real projects while they are in progress, enabling them to reflect collectively on ways to improve processes. This action-reflection cycle is repeated as necessary until the improvement goal is achieved. Consistent with the principles of multi-level learning discussed in Chapter 2, cross-project improvement is focused on eliminating waste, delivering as fast as possible, and seeing the whole with the help of an objective, substantively neutral third-party coach. Questions include: What patterns are emerging from project retrospectives that appear to be affecting many projects? Which improvements that were made by specific teams can be shared across other projects? Which cross-project activities are consuming the most time and resources, and what can be done to make them more effective?

Both the multi-level learning coach and the program manager or program management office (PMO) provide an important function. As noted in Chapter 3, the multi-level learning coach has no decision-making authority and serves as a substantively neutral third party. She works with the program management office to plan and conduct regular action-reflection cycles with project managers and other subject-matter experts from across the project organization. A key function of the PMO at this level is to incorporate improvements and innovations into the organization's processes, systems, and methodologies so that future teams can use them. Chapter 4 discussed in detail how PMO leaders broker knowledge in this way, enabling the organization to incorporate ongoing improvements in ways that enable systems-level learning.

Having covered the goals and roles required for cross-project improvement, we now turn to the steps required to make it happen. As shown in Figure 6.1, these steps include (1) plan and conduct the cross-project

FIGURE 6.1
Steps for Level 2: Cross-Project Improvement

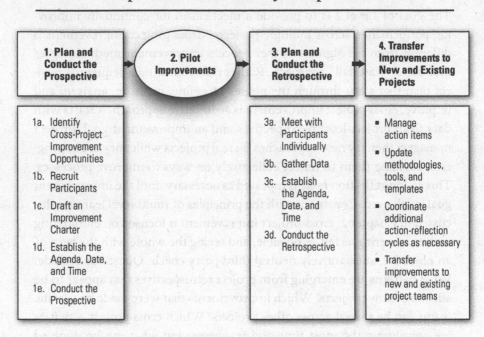

prospective, (2) pilot improvements, (3) plan and conduct the cross-project retrospective, and (4) transfer improvements to new and existing projects. Coverage of each of these steps follows, beginning with Step 1.

STEP 1: PLAN AND CONDUCT THE PROSPECTIVE

This step consists of the following activities: (a) Identify a high-priority problem area, (b) recruit participants, (c) draft an improvement charter, (d) establish an agenda, date, and time, and (e) conduct a cross-project prospective.

Step 1a: Identify Cross-Project Improvement Opportunities

There are many ways to identify opportunities for improvement across multiple projects. In environments in which many similar projects are happening concurrently, the PMO leader or program manager may find activities that consistently run into problems. Common themes or patterns that point to similar causes may arise from project retrospectives. For example, a research organization was finding that different managers were initiating cross-functional projects that required many of the same people. Moreover, these projects had conflicting objectives. After several projects were cancelled abruptly, the management team said, "Enough!" and enlisted the PMO leader's help in solving the problem. The PMO leader then gathered a group of project managers from across the organization to develop a revised approach for launching projects that would ensure that the right people were involved at each step to minimize conflicts in the project portfolio. The new approach was implemented successfully, in part because those people who were required to make the change happen were involved in developing the new solution.

In another example of a cross-project improvement success, a different company's PMO leader found that while most projects were delivering on time and within expectations, systems testing had been consistently taking an inordinate amount of time and resources. Moreover, feedback from project retrospectives was pointing to misunderstandings and missed expectations on software requirements. As a result, the PMO leader held a prospective session focused on improving the requirements development process.

Step 1b: Recruit Participants

The people to recruit for cross-project improvement efforts, as for any organizational change, should be those who can both benefit and contribute the most. Since the approach requires people to take action on real projects, it is important to select people who have a degree of influence over a project team's activities, so that they can plan and execute new approaches. Project managers will often be in this position, although there may be other people with specific subject-matter expertise who could prove equally valuable. It is also important that the people selected be about to undertake the process being improved. For example, if the focus is on improving the requirements development process, then people who will be involved in gathering requirements in the upcoming period should be recruited. To best utilize the talents of those in the organization and to develop improvements that make a difference, it is also important to recruit people who are interested in improving future results. This motivation may be derived from a desire to avoid additional frustration on future efforts, or the area may be something that they are intrinsically interested in improving.

Step 1c: Draft an Improvement Charter

Once a focus area has been chosen and interested parties have been recruited, the PMO, in consultation with the participants, drafts a brief "charter" that covers the following: the "business case" and associated problem statement, the business objectives or goals to be achieved, key milestones, team members, scope, and costs and benefits. Data from multiple project-level retrospectives should be used to frame the business case and problem statement. Questions to consider in developing the charter include: What first brought the problem to our attention? What impact has it already had across projects? What evidence is there that this is a substantive problem that is worth addressing? What are the perceived root causes of the problem? What will happen if it is not addressed? Figure 6.2 provides a template that can be used to develop an improvement charter.

Step 1d: Establish an Agenda, Date, and Time

Like that for the project team prospective, the agenda should enable the improvement team to clarify its goals and roles with respect to making improvements and developing its approach. The following questions should be considered:

1. What is the problem, and what is our objective in relation to solving it?
2. What are the roles and responsibilities of each individual involved?
3. What are the time and budget constraints?
4. What are possible improvements that can be made and on which projects will they be piloted?

The improvement charter serves as the primary document for use in the meeting's discussion. The PMO or program leader, in consultation with the

FIGURE 6.2
Improvement Charter Template

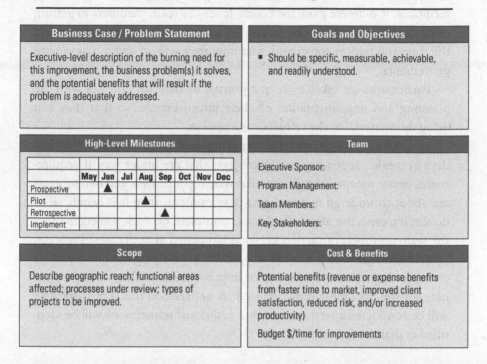

Business Case / Problem Statement
Executive-level description of the burning need for this improvement, the business problem(s) it solves, and the potential benefits that will result if the problem is adequately addressed.

Goals and Objectives
▪ Should be specific, measurable, achievable, and readily understood.

High-Level Milestones

	May	Jun	Jul	Aug	Sep	Oct	Nov	Dec
Prospective		▲						
Pilot				▲				
Retrospective					▲			
Implement								

Team
Executive Sponsor:
Program Management:
Team Members:
Key Stakeholders:

Scope
Describe geographic reach; functional areas affected; processes under review; types of projects to be improved.

Cost & Benefits
Potential benefits (revenue or expense benefits from faster time to market, improved client satisfaction, reduced risk, and/or increased productivity)
Budget $/time for improvements

coach, will need to use his judgment to determine how much time should be dedicated to each of these areas. In all cases, ground rules for group discussions are developed or reviewed (see Chapter 3). Before the session ends, the PMO leader and the coach help participants get clarity concerning how they can define and implement improvements on their projects after the meeting. Team members will need authority and influence with their respective teams so that they can work with them to implement the new approaches. As this requires real work on real projects, the organization needs to provide the latitude to enable improvements to be made.

Step 1e: Conduct the Prospective

The prospective may be led by the coach, the program manager, or the PMO leader, depending on their level of skill and availability. As discussed in Chapters 2 and 3, respectively, the facilitator needs to be skilled in effective group intervention and the principles of multi-level learning. The coach may intervene when required to keep the group on track, while the facilitator, if different from the coach, leads the team members in getting clarity concerning the problem and the objectives, their respective roles, the time and budget constraints, and how they will go about making improvements.

Participants are asked to keep a journal of their experiences with the planning and implementation of their improvements so that they can bring this material to the retrospective session.

Upon closing the prospective, the group will agree to meet after a few days or weeks, depending on the projects that are under way. If requirements development is the process that is being improved, and two projects are about to undergo requirements development, then it is beneficial to do the retrospective after this phase is complete on each project, so that the team members can reflect on what happened in both cases. Typically, project managers and teams are responsible for creating their own project plans, so they can build in and pilot improvements as they do their planning for the upcoming time period. It is understood that a retrospective will be conducted afterward, and that additional refinements will be identified at that time.

STEP 2: PILOT IMPROVEMENTS

After the prospective, the participants return to their respective project teams to plan the deployment of improvements aimed at solving the problems outlined in the improvement charter. This can be done in several ways, depending on the projects in the pipeline and the specific organizational environment. Project managers may choose to deploy multiple solutions, or it may be more practical to focus on just one or two. In addition, it may be necessary for the improvement team to meet several times to collect more data, identify root causes, or develop new tools, templates, or solutions before changes can be implemented on new projects. The PMO leader and the coach collaborate to determine the most effective approach given the size of the problem, the magnitude of the benefits that can be achieved, and the amount of time that people are able to dedicate.

While improvements are being developed and implemented, team members may want to keep a journal to record their thinking and other events that occur along the way in preparation for the cross-project retrospective, the planning and conducting of which is covered next.

STEP 3: PLAN AND CONDUCT THE RETROSPECTIVE

After improvements have been made, either on one project or across multiple projects, the PMO leader and the coach work together to plan and conduct a cross-project retrospective. This step consists of the following activities: (a) Meet with participants individually, (b) gather data, (c) establish the agenda, date, and time, and (d) conduct the retrospective.

Step 3a: Meet with Participants Individually

The PMO leader or program manager may want to meet with group members individually to provide support as they plan and implement potential improvements for their respective projects, and he may work with project managers, sponsors, or others to help pave the way for the use of improved approaches.

Step 3b: Gather Data

Prior to the retrospective, the PMO leader asks each participant to develop a timeline of the steps her team took over the course of its work. The timeline should also include any significant events that may have occurred. This will be brought to the session and shared with other members of the group. As with the project retrospective, it is also useful to have factual data related to actual person-hours, actual output (lines of code, for example), and the number of defects, delays, or schedule slips that occurred. Having these data will help in establishing a fact base for evaluating the impact of improvements. Examples of the questions for data collection might include the following:

1. What was the calendar time and number of person-hours required at each stage?

2. What were the schedule slips on the project, and when did they occur?
3. How many defects were found at each stage, what was their severity?
4. What are the customer, internal client, or sponsor's perceptions regarding progress and results?

Step 3c: Establish the Agenda, Date, and Time for the Retrospective

As discussed in Chapter 2, the purpose of the cross-project retrospective is to reflect on the steps that teams take to accomplish their work. The agenda for this is similar to that for the project retrospective, except that the focus is on the steps taken on more than one project. The retrospective should result in answers to the following questions:

1. What was the problem identified at the outset, and what was our objective for improvement?
2. What actual results occurred after implementing these improvements? What were the perceptions of the project team members, internal clients, customers, and other key stakeholders with regard to their effectiveness?
3. What were the primary causes or determinants of these results and perceptions, whether favorable or unfavorable?
4. What worked well that we don't want to forget?
5. What improvements will be carried forward into future activities, and how will the knowledge transfer be accomplished?

The coach will design an agenda that addresses these questions based on his style preferences, skills, and abilities. Like the prospective, the meeting should start by reviewing the ground rules for group interaction, including Kerth's Prime Directive (see Chapter 3 for a more detailed discussion). In addition, the following agenda items should also be considered:

1. *Review the improvement charter.* This should be brief and to the point.
2. *Share timelines.* In the planning discussions, group members were asked to bring a timeline depicting the steps their team took and any significant events that occurred. Allocate time for each person to discuss

her timeline, significant data, improvements the she found useful, and what she might do differently next time.

3. *Identify innovations.* Working from their respective timelines, the group members identify practices that improved results and should be incorporated into future projects. Questions to ask here include: What worked well that we don't want to forget? What did we learn from this?

4. *Define additional improvements.* The group discusses additional improvement opportunities that might be incorporated into future project plans. If time allows, the list should be prioritized to collect the team's perspectives on which ones will have the most impact. Criteria for prioritization might include impact on calendar time, work time, customer satisfaction, quality, and/or employee development.

5. *Determine if another iteration is required.* Before ending the session, the group, in consultation with the PMO leader, should decide whether or not another iteration of improvement is required. It is likely that significant problems will require multiple iterations to generate sustainable improvement.

Norm Kerth (2001) and Esther Derby and Diana Larsen (2006) provide a number of additional tools that can be used for process retrospectives, including (for those familiar with quality tools) force field analysis, five whys, and the fishbone diagram, any of which can be useful depending on the situation at hand.

Step 3d: Conduct the Process Retrospective

The retrospective is facilitated by the coach. As a skilled facilitator of learning and improvement, he helps the group members look back on their respective projects in ways that promote valid information, free and informed choice, and internal commitment to changes. He helps people collaborate effectively, reminding people about tools such as TALK, the Ladder of Inference, and collaborative conflict resolution (see Chapter 3 for a detailed discussion of how and under what circumstances the coach should intervene to keep the group on track). When retrospectives are conducted effectively, groups will become increasingly skilled in reflecting and improving in ways that make substantial cross-project improvement possible.

STEP 4: TRANSFER IMPROVEMENTS TO NEW AND EXISTING PROJECTS

After the retrospective session ends, much of the work begins for the PMO or the program manager. In collaboration with group members, she does the following:

- Document and follow-up on the action items from the retrospective.
- Refine and augment methodologies, tools, and templates.
- Coordinate additional cross-project improvement sessions as required.
- Transfer improvements to new and existing projects.

As noted in Chapter 4, PMO leaders and their teams should attempt to communicate "process knowledge"—knowledge about how a team can go about solving specific problems. Process knowledge enables a broader number of people to use the resulting insights, whereas project deliverables alone are often project-specific and may lack broader utility.

If key stakeholders were involved in the previous steps and feel that their time was well spent, encouraging the use of the improved practices on future projects may not be difficult. That's because project managers have already been involved in developing improvements for problems that matter to them. They will have utilized valid information to make free and informed choices about how to improve future project work, leading to greater levels of internal commitment and broader adoption. Those involved with developing the process improvements can themselves become evangelists for their transfer to other projects.

CONCLUSION

Cross-project improvements enable organizations with many concurrent projects to spread innovations across teams, creating a multiplier effect that leads to improvement in multiple projects simultaneously. Consistent with the principles of multi-level learning, cross-project improvements help project organizations deliver faster, improve customer satisfaction, reduce waste, and empower teams to learn and improve. As a knowledge broker, the PMO facilitates continuous improvement by incorporating cross-project innovations into the group's processes, methodologies, tools, templates, and systems so that future projects can benefit from the resulting insights.

In the next chapter, we cover how the multi-level learning coach and the PMO leader work with senior managers to facilitate alignment between the organization's strategy and the project portfolio as a whole.

7 | FACILITATING LEVEL 3: STRATEGIC PORTFOLIO ALIGNMENT

As representatives of investors, shareholders, or the public in general, senior leaders are responsible for establishing the organization's mission and vision, as well as its strategic objectives and plans. These objectives may include enhancing revenue growth, improving productivity, increasing customer loyalty, or delivering higher levels of service. To accomplish these aims, strategies must often be translated into discrete projects and programs that must be executed effectively in order to produce the business transformation desired. These initiatives often represent significant investments, and may include such things as developing and launching innovative new products, making operations and technology improvements that increase quality and productivity, upgrading supply chain technologies, executing mergers and acquisitions that grow the firm's market share and increase its competitiveness, or finding ways to deliver business results to customers faster and more effectively than ever before.

While senior teams and their designates are responsible for formulating successful strategies, these strategies will almost always need to be enhanced, adjusted, and modified as conditions "on the ground" change and new information becomes available. The reality is that strategies require continual refinement to ensure that they are effective and relevant. Adapting strategies to changing conditions is not a sign of weakness, vulnerability, or lack of determination. Rather, when effective learning mechanisms are in place, adaptation is a sign of strength, competitiveness, and strategic agility that will enable the organization to utilize its resources more efficiently in achieving its strategic aims. The benefits include reduced risk of failure, more efficient use of scarce investment capital, and wise deployment of the organization's top talent.

This chapter provides information on how the multi-level learning coach and the program management office (PMO) can help senior teams maintain alignment between the organization's strategic objectives and its overall project and program portfolio. The chapter begins with a discussion of the goals of this component of multi-level learning and the respective roles of the PMO, the coach, and the senior management team. The chapter then moves to a step-by-step approach for facilitating improvement at this level.

OVERVIEW OF LEVEL 3:
STRATEGIC PORTFOLIO ALIGNMENT

The goal of Level 3 of the multi-level learning approach is to provide a mechanism by which the senior management team can optimize the value of the organization's overall project portfolio by selecting and nurturing the right projects and programs at the right time with the right amount of resources. Consistent with the principles of multi-level learning discussed in Chapter 2, the senior management team reflects on ways to eliminate waste, deliver as fast as possible, and see the whole, while welcoming new insights, empowering team learning, using a third-party coach, and reflecting at three levels (project, process, and strategy). Questions include: Which projects and programs are required to enable us to achieve our intended strategy in the most cost-effective way? To what extent are the current projects moving us toward our objectives? What adjustments need to be made to ensure that we achieve our intended results? What actions need to be taken, and at which levels of the organization?

Both the multi-level learning coach and the PMO play crucial roles in helping the senior team learn, adapt, and improve the project portfolio. As noted in Chapter 3, the multi-level learning coach has no decision-making authority and serves as a substantively neutral third party. She works with the PMO to plan and conduct prospective and retrospective sessions with the leadership team before and after each iteration or phase of the strategic program to clarify what needs to be done and to reflect on what was actually accomplished.

As at all levels of multi-level learning, the PMO leader—or the program leader serving in this role—brokers the process by coordinating, translating, and aligning the senior team's efforts with those of other teams and communities of practice, which include project teams, business units, and other functional departments. A key function of the PMO at this level is to provide the senior team with information about how projects and programs are performing, not only with respect to their cost, time, and quality goals, but also with respect to their effectiveness in the eyes of the project's customers and internal clients.

The respective roles of the senior management team will depend on the strategic objectives at hand, yet obtaining full consensus on portfolio decisions is critical. The CIO, for example, may take a more prominent decision-making role on initiatives that involve technology transformation. Likewise, the HR leader might do so for programs related to changes in professional development, compensation, or performance evaluation practices. As discussed in Chapter 3, however, to ensure that each team member is internally committed and feels responsible for the group's choices, it is desirable to have consensus on decisions related to the organization's project portfolio. Therefore, using the RACI decision-making model discussed in Chapter 3, the CIO and HR leaders in these situations might be R, or recommenders, while the other members of the senior team may be A, or approvers. As most of us know from our experience in organizations, both the CIO and the HR leader will need full cooperation and commitment from others, particularly if these changes have the potential to be transformational.

Having covered the goals and roles required, we now turn to the steps required. As shown in Figure 7.1, these steps include (1) plan and conduct the strategy prospective, (2) execute the strategy, (3) plan and conduct the strategy retrospective, and (4) update the project portfolio and capture action items. Coverage of each of these steps follows, beginning with Step 1, plan and conduct the prospective.

FIGURE 7.1
Steps for Level 3: Strategic Portfolio Alignment

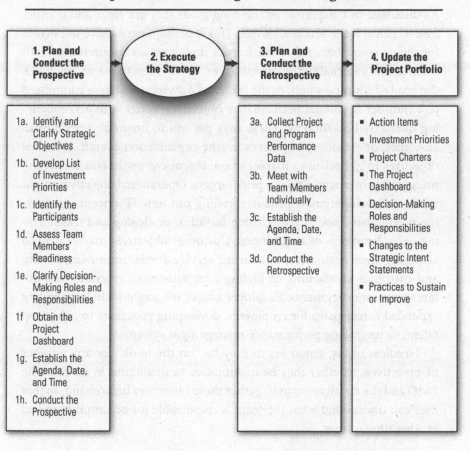

STEP 1: PLAN AND CONDUCT THE PROSPECTIVE

Before conducting the first prospective with the senior management team, the coach and the PMO work together to (a) identify and clarify strategic objectives, (b) develop a list of investment priorities, (c) identify participants, (d) assess team members' readiness, (e) outline an initial understanding of roles and responsibilities, (f) collect information related to key performance indicators, (g) establish an agenda, date, and time, and (h) conduct the prospective.

Step 1a: Identify and Clarify Strategic Objectives

As discussed in Chapter 3, establishing goals that are clear and conflict free is critical for teams at all levels. This is perhaps even more important for senior teams because of the impact they have on communities both internal and external to the organization. More often than not, the CEO, the head of a business unit, or the leader of a division will have committed to a number of annual performance objectives, often with accompanying quarterly breakdowns. These may pertain to financial, operational, customer, or employee objectives for the organization overall. Financial objectives might relate to market share, revenue growth, cost reduction, margin improvement, or share price targets. Operational objectives might relate to developing new products, rolling out new IT systems, improving productivity, opening or closing facilities, or closing and transforming units, locations, or acquisitions. Customer objectives may pertain to acquiring new customers, enhancing service levels, improving loyalty and customer satisfaction, or finding new sources of revenue from different customer segments. Employee objectives might include providing expanded career paths for employees, developing programs to rotate top talent, or upgrading performance management systems.

Needless to say, senior teams may be "on the hook" for any number of objectives, whether they be quantitative or qualitative in nature. The PMO and the coach attempt to gather these objectives beforehand, so that they can understand what the team is responsible for accomplishing and in what time frames.

Step 1b: Develop a List of Investment Priorities

The PMO may also have developed—or will want to develop—a list of "investment priorities," or initiatives that represent potential projects and programs that will enable the organization to execute its strategy. These initiatives may be vague initially, and funds may also be allotted to each "bucket." Where possible, the PMO leader should obtain this information, as it will serve as a jumping-off point for establishing project and program priorities. As shown in Figure 7.2, this list should include the name of each potential initiative, a problem or opportunity statement, the scope,

FIGURE 7.2
Investment Priorities

Rank	Category	Initiative	Problem Statement	Objectives	Scope
1	Marketing	New Customer Acquisition Strategy	Sed ut perspiciatis unde omnis iste natus error sit voluptatem accusantium doloremque laudantium, totam rem aperiam, eaque ipsa quae ab illo inventore veritatis et quasi architecto beatae vitae dicta sunt explicabo. N emo enim ipsam voluptatem qui	Establish new sales channel for product enhancements	Sed ut perspiciatis unde omnis iste natus error sit voluptatem accusantium doloremque laudantium, totam rem aperiam, eaque ipsa quae ab illo inventore veritatis et quasi architecto beatae vitae dicta sunt explicabo. N emo enim ipsam voluptatem quia volu
2	Product Development	New Product Launch	Sed ut perspiciatis unde omnis iste natus error sit voluptatem accusantium doloremque laudantium, totam rem aperiam, eaque ipsa quae ab illo inventore veritatis et quasi architecto beatae vitae dicta sunt explicabo. N emo enim ipsam voluptatem qui	Launch product upgrade in fourth quarter	Sed ut perspiciatis unde omnis iste natus error sit voluptatem accusantium doloremque laudantium, totam rem aperiam, eaque ipsa quae ab illo inventore veritatis et quasi architecto beatae vitae dicta sunt explicabo. N emo enim ipsam voluptatem quia volu
3	IT	Enterprise Software Implementation	Sed ut perspiciatis unde omnis iste natus error sit voluptatem accusantium doloremque laudantium, totam rem aperiam, eaque ipsa quae ab illo inventore veritatis et quasi architecto beatae vitae dicta sunt explicabo. N emo enim ipsam voluptatem quia volu	Complete the process and systems improvements for back office operations	Sed ut perspiciatis unde omnis iste natus error sit voluptatem accusantium doloremque laudantium, totam rem aperiam, eaque ipsa quae ab illo inventore veritatis et quasi architecto beatae vitae dicta sunt explicabo. N emo enim ipsam voluptatem quia volu
4	Product Development	New Customer Web Site	Sed ut perspiciatis unde omnis iste natus error sit voluptatem accusantium doloremque laudantium, totam rem aperiam, eaque ipsa quae ab illo inventore veritatis et quasi architecto beatae vitae dicta sunt explicabo. N emo enim ipsam voluptatem qui	Provide customers with new and enhanced web site by third quarter	Sed ut perspiciatis unde omnis iste natus error sit voluptatem accusantium doloremque laudantium, totam rem aperiam, eaque ipsa quae ab illo inventore veritatis et quasi architecto beatae vitae dicta sunt explicabo. N emo enim ipsam voluptatem quia volu
5	Sales	Streamline the Business Development Process	Sed ut perspiciatis unde omnis iste natus error sit voluptatem accusantium doloremque laudantium, totam rem aperiam, eaque ipsa quae ab illo inventore veritatis et quasi architecto beatae vitae dicta sunt explicabo. N emo enim ipsam voluptatem qui	Reduce new sales closing cycle by 30% before year end	Sed ut perspiciatis unde omnis iste natus error sit voluptatem accusantium doloremque laudantium, totam rem aperiam, eaque ipsa quae ab illo inventore veritatis et quasi architecto beatae vitae dicta sunt explicabo. N emo enim ipsam voluptatem quia volu

the potential objectives, the amount of funds allocated, and the initiative's rank in relation to other initiatives. It may also be useful to develop criteria for tanking these investment priorities against one another. For example, they may be evaluated against such criteria as their ability to improve the customer experience, reduce costs, move the organization toward its intended strategy, or improve employee engagement.

Step 1c: Identify the Participants

Usually, who should attend the senior team prospective is obvious. It may be a direct reflection of the organization chart. More often than not, it includes the leader of the organization and her direct reports. In some situations, however, the senior team may need additional expertise, either from within the organization or from outside. The coach and the PMO leader should ensure that these people are included as well, even if only for the specific portion of the meeting that applies to their domain of expertise or decision-making authority. For example, the company may have signed a multiyear outsourcing agreement with a key strategic business partner. A representative of this group might attend if decisions that require the partner's commitment and leadership are to be made. Keep in mind that while a more junior person may be required for her expertise, this individual may, depending on the climate and culture, be "outgunned" or intimidated, leading to distortions in her ability to contribute effectively. This is something that the coach should note beforehand, and perhaps discuss with other team members prior to the meeting.

Step 1d: Assess Team Members' Readiness

Prior to the prospective, and after identifying the goals and the attendees, the coach will want to hold a short discussion with each team member to describe the purpose of the session and get his feedback on the agenda. It is at this time that the coach can both clarify her role and ask questions that will help to clarify goals, roles, and procedures. The coach may identify potential conflicts and, as discussed in Chapter 4, may need to ask questions beforehand that help her understand the underlying needs of each member.

Step 1e: Clarify Decision-Making Roles and Responsibilities

The PMO leader will want to develop an initial draft of the decision-making roles in relation to decisions about the project portfolio. The RACI tool described in Chapter 3 can be a useful tool for this purpose. Certain members may be recommenders and others approvers for key decisions, such as which projects should be launched, how these projects will be managed, and which projects should be cancelled or repurposed. As discussed previously, it is especially important to have consensus on portfolio decisions that affect multiple groups. Figure 7.3 shows an example of a RACI chart for one organization's project portfolio decisions.

Step 1f: Obtain the Project Dashboard

Many organizations have a "dashboard" that provides updated information on the status of projects and programs and how they are performing. As discussed in Chapter 4, the PMO is often responsible for putting this information together. Each project may be rated red, yellow, or green in traffic light fashion, with red indicating that a project is in trouble and yellow that it is in danger. Red indicates that it has slipped in delivering on its objectives, time frames, or other expectations. There may also be an update on when the next review or "tollgate" is to occur for each project, and where each project stands in terms of its timeline and milestones. An example of a simple project dashboard is shown in Figure 7.4.

Step 1g: Establish the Agenda, Date, and Time for the Strategy Prospective

Depending on where the organization is beginning, a strategy prospective can take anywhere from two to three hours to two to three days. At the outset of a major strategic initiative or business transformation, the team may need to have a few days off-site to set its direction for the upcoming time period. In other situations, the organization may have already been reviewing the project portfolio regularly as part of a project review process, reducing the time required. Based on the information collected in the earlier steps, and with knowledge of effective group processes as

FIGURE 7.3
RACI Chart for Project Portfolio Decisions

Decision	Phase	COO	Mgt Team Member	Sponsor	PMO	Project Mgr	Key Stakeholders
Create charter for new project idea	I	A	A	R	R	R	C
Go/no-go on project charter and move to Discover phase	II	A	C	R	R	C	I
Go/no-go on move to Develop phase	III	A	A	R	R	C	I
Go/no-go on move to Doit phase	IV	A	A	R	R	C	C
Close out project	V	A	A	C	R	C	I

A = APPROVE— a person who must sign off or veto a decision before it is implemented or selected from options developed by the R role; accountable for the quality of the decision.

R = RESPONSIBLE—the person who takes the initiative in the particular area, develops the alternatives, analyzes the situation, makes the initial recommendation, and is accountable if nothing happens in the area.

C = CONSULTED—a person who must be consulted prior to a decision being reached but with no veto power.

I = INFORMED—a person who must be notified after a decision, but before it is publicly announced; someone who needs to know the outcome for other related tasks but need not give input.

covered in Chapter 3, the coach will develop an agenda, date, and time for the prospective, in consultation with senior decision makers and the PMO leader. Each prospective may have a different emphasis depending on what stage in a strategy or program's life cycle it is in and how much experience the senior team has with these types of sessions. Yet regardless of where the team members are with regard to their progress or experience, the purpose of the prospective is to answer and come to agreement on the following questions for the upcoming period, phase, or iteration. These questions serve as the outline of the agenda:

1. What is the team's strategic intent for the upcoming time period?
2. What projects and programs are required to achieve the strategic intent?
3. What are the roles and responsibilities of each individual with respect to making this happen?
4. What are the key performance indicators that will enable us to know whether or not we have accomplished what we set out to achieve?

FIGURE 7.4
Example Project Portfolio Dashboard

Headlines
- Projects generally progressing; charters and milestones refined
- Significant change in product/service model unlikely for January
- Must determine product/service strategy for 1st Qtr implementation

Issues
- Do we have a clear and compelling statement about the new product and service strategy?
- How will Project Firestorm help us achieve the product strategy?
- To which quarterly cycle will the Market Research project apply?

Project	Sponsor/PM	Def	Dis	Dev	Do	Tollgate	RAG	Reason for Rating
Product Strategy	M. Rotland / N. Jones				*Out of Scope*	8/8		Decisions required for January launch.
Future Customer Research	R. Feldman / N. James				*Out of Scope*	8/15		Review for integration with Product Development.
Transformation Strategy	M. Forster / M. Forster				*Out of Scope*	8/8		Question as to how outputs will be prioritized and decisioned.
PM Process Improvement	T. Fireman / J. Jones					8/8		Should be transitioned to steering committee member.
Customer Loyalty Program Launch	T. Fireman / D. Porter				*Out of Scope*	8/8		Recommendations not yet translated to project charters.
Sales and Service Strategy	J. Rigger / P. Ryan					8/8		Should be transitioned to steering committee member.
Web Strategy	M. Wolfman / S. Sintre					8/29		Project charter refined; plan in progress. Requirements approval required.
Financial Process Reengineering	M. Jackman / M. Rotter					8/29		Should be transitioned to steering committee member.
Managerial Skill Upgrade	T. Fireman / M. Hyman					8/8		Project charter needs approval.
Talent Management Program **New**	T. Jackson / J. Minster					9/26		Project planning in progress; staffing completed.

Legend: ▨ Last reporting period (7/18)   ▪ Since last reporting period   ☐ To be completed   ▨ Out of Scope

Ideas

Priority	Project	Charter Assigned to	By When	Governing Body	Status
1 **New**	Sales Forecasting Process Redesign	J. Ryan M. Forman	8/8,	SC	On track
2	Customer Relationship Management System	E. Sintre	8/15	IT	Delayed
3	Financial / Supply Chain Integration	TBD	TBD	SC	TBD
4 **New**	Product Strategy	TBD	TBD	SC	TBD

Completed Projects

Project	Project Manager
Communication Strategy	P. Ryan

On Hold/Pending

Project	Reason
Workforce Transition **New**	Awaiting review & agreed-upon strategy

The team's strategic intent is a series of statements about how it intends to move toward achieving its strategic objectives. Examples include "Identify three core processes that can be moved to a shared services model," "Launch new product A," and "Identify growth opportunities that will enable product B to gain over 20 percent market share." Crafting these statements will enable the senior team to get a handle on its overall strategy for the upcoming time period, enabling it to separate the details of each project or program from the larger strategic picture. This may be done in a top-down or a bottom-up way, depending on where the organization is beginning. If investment priorities have yet to be translated into projects and programs, then this may serve as a starting point for crafting statements of strategic intent. Where there are already projects in the pipeline, it may be useful to categorize related projects into families of initiatives and "roll up" the strategic intent for each family. This would represent a "bottom-up" approach.

In all cases, before addressing these topics in sequential fashion, the coach first facilitates a discussion about ground rules for group discussions (see Chapter 3) and ensures that time is allocated to this task on the agenda, particularly for the first prospective. In situations in which the team needs to develop statements of strategic intent and develop project and program objectives from scratch, these topics will obviously require more time on the agenda. The PMO leader can add tremendous value by drafting the agenda items in advance so that the team can react, modify, and agree rather than create them on the fly. However, while the PMO leader may have developed an initial list of roles and responsibilities in Step 1E, these will need to be agreed upon in the group session, and time should be dedicated to this task as well. Finally, time should be allocated to determining key performance indicators for each statement of strategic intent. For example, how will the group measure whether or not the introduction of a new product was successful? Most organizations will have measures that they use, such as customer satisfaction surveys, returns, calls to the call center, and other such actions that indicate whether or not the organization was successful in achieving its strategic intent.

Step 1h: Conduct the Prospective

In Chapter 3, we discussed the importance of having clarified and conflict-free goals, roles, and procedures. Getting clarity concerning strategic intent, projects and programs, roles, and key performance indicators is the primary goal of the strategy prospective. Unlike the retrospective, which may place people in a defensive posture and therefore needs to be facilitated by the multi-level learning coach, the prospective may be led by the PMO leader or a person in a similar role, as long as this person is skilled in the use of effective group intervention and the principles of multi-level learning described in Chapters 2 and 3, respectively. The coach may intervene when required to keep the group on track, while the PMO leader or the coach leads the team in getting clarity concerning its strategic intent, projects and programs, roles and responsibilities, and key performance indicators. Doing this sets the stage for the group to take action in the next iteration or phase, knowing that in a few weeks' time, it will reflect as a group on what worked, what didn't, and what needs to be sustained or changed the next time around. Where possible, participants are asked to keep a journal of their experiences so that they can bring this material to the retrospective session.

STEP 2: EXECUTE THE STRATEGY

After gaining agreement on the organization's key strategic objectives, projects, programs, and key performance indicators, the senior team begins working the plan. They provide resources, direction, and support that enables the broader organization to understand the overall goals, their respective roles, and the key initiatives planned for the upcoming time period.

We next address how the coach and the PMO together plan and conduct the portfolio retrospective.

STEP 3: PLAN AND CONDUCT THE
PORTFOLIO RETROSPECTIVE

After a period of time, anywhere from a month to no more than a quarter, the senior management team reassembles to look back on what results were actually delivered across the projects and programs in the portfolio, and to what extent they have achieved their strategic intent for that time period. The portfolio retrospective is different from a standard project portfolio review. It is not meant to replace it. Standard portfolio reviews are informational. They provide the senior team with updates on what projects and programs have delivered, their status, and what needs to happen next to either get them back on track or keep them running. The focus is on teams getting feedback from the key decision makers. The portfolio retrospective adds another dimension. It asks the senior team to reflect on what decisions and actions need to be taken to achieve the firm's business strategy and how the projects and programs are doing with respect to achieving the strategy. The portfolio retrospective enables senior leaders to reflect on the fitness of the portfolio itself, without the added complexity of "saving face" in front of subordinates or others at more junior levels. Whether good or bad, most organizations have cultures that put pressure on leaders to know exactly what they should be doing at any given time and to position themselves relative to others in the hierarchy. Conducting the portfolio retrospective with those responsible for formulating strategy can lead to thinking and breakthroughs that would not be possible otherwise.

As for the prospective session, the coach works with the PMO to lay the groundwork. The coach facilitates the session, helping the team to reflect productively by intervening when necessary to encourage an effective group process. In this step, the PMO leader and coach work together to (A) collect performance data, (B) meet with team members individually, (C) establish the agenda, date, and time, and (D) conduct the retrospective.

Step 3a: Collect Project and Program Performance Data

Most PMOs have established status reporting systems and portfolio dashboards that provide updated information on each project and how it's tracking against the schedule, the budget, resource consumption, and possibly even some measures of quality, such as customer feedback or the number of bugs or defects identified on technology-related projects. Some PMOs even have a "health check" or internal audits for projects and programs to ensure compliance with government regulations or standard operating procedures. All these data can be collected, reviewed, and summarized.

While a great deal of data may be available to the PMO, those data may or may not be useful for determining how the organization is tracking against its strategic objectives. This is especially true when projects have long durations and use a "waterfall" approach that defers getting feedback from customers or end users until late in the project. Initiatives with long life cycles may remain "green" for some time. By the time end users and customers have the opportunity to see the results, it may be months down the road. A project that was going just fine can suddenly be delayed for an indefinite period of time, creating disappointment and questions about why the problems weren't anticipated earlier.

As discussed in Chapter 2, the principles of multi-level learning encourage quick iterations of project delivery that place working end products in users' hands sooner, so that teams can learn, improve, and deliver what customers actually need and want. Measures of on-time performance and budget variance are clearly useful as intermediate measures, but short iterations that give customers and internal clients the ability to offer their perceptions reduces waste and focuses resources on the right areas sooner rather than later. Of course, short iterations are an ideal, and are not always possible for all types of projects.

Perhaps the most useful tool for gauging strategic objectives is the benefits realization schedule. A good benefits realization schedule provides updated revenue, expense, and capital investment numbers for each project and program. The schedule depicts the benefits actually delivered to the business, if any, along with a forecast of those to be delivered in the future. It provides time frames for when revenues and expenses are expected, their magnitude, and perhaps even the probabilities associated with various targets. In addition, it provides the capital outlays, both actual and expected, for each project and program. This information is made available for both "drilling down" and "rolling up" so that decision makers can see how they are tracking against quantitative financial goals.

The benefits realization schedule, or at the very least the beginning of one, should be developed and provided, along with the project dashboard, before the retrospective so that group members can review and absorb the information beforehand.

Step 3b: Meet with Team Members Individually

Prior to the session, the coach will need to speak individually with each manager to do the following:

1. Describe the retrospective process and its benefits.
2. Ask the manager what topics he feels need to be addressed.
3. Determine whether there are areas of particular sensitivity.

4. Ask him to collect artifacts—previous dashboards, project and program charters, strategy documents, product designs, business plans, contracts, project and program schedules, previous status reports, and so on—that are relevant for discussion in the retrospective.

These conversations, particularly for the first senior team retrospective, enable the coach to build rapport, prepare an agenda, and identify potential "hot buttons" that may lead to defensive routines, avoidance, or blame. They also provide an opportunity to talk about what each member needs to bring to the session in the form of artifacts. These may be drawn from e-mail exchanges, meeting notes, presentations, project reviews, and so on, and they will be used in the retrospective to focus the discussion. They serve as a means for communicating agreement and focusing on actual events, so that each member of the group is able to provide perspectives on the things that she feels are most important for discussion. This helps to both refresh memories and keep the focus on actual events.

Step 3c: Establish the Agenda, Date, and Time

As discussed in Chapter 2, the purpose of the retrospective is to reflect on actual results so that the team can plan actions that improve future results. The objectives of the retrospective are to answer the following questions:

1. What was our strategic intent for the previous time period?
2. What were the actual results that were delivered by projects and programs?
3. What were the primary causes of these results, whether favorable or unfavorable?
4. How did our actions and decisions at the project portfolio level lead to these outcomes?
5. Which projects and programs should be initiated, closed, or repositioned, and why?
6. What other actions need to be taken to accomplish our strategic objectives?

The coach will design his agenda to achieve these objectives based on the planning discussions and his style preferences for how to accomplish them based on his unique skills and abilities. As with the prospective, the meeting should start by establishing or reviewing ground rules for group interaction (see Chapter 3 for a more detailed discussion). In addition, the following agenda items should also be considered:

1. *Review statements of strategic intent.* The group reviews the statements of strategic intent developed for the prospective session. This should be brief and to the point. Because these statements are supported by individual project and program objectives, a brief review of these objectives may also be appropriate.

2. *Share artifacts.* In the planning discussions, group members were asked to bring important artifacts to the session, including key decisions, strategy documents, project schedules, contracts, and so on. Allocate time for each person to discuss the artifacts she brought as she sees fit.

3. *Develop a timeline.* Facilitate the development of a timeline of important events that occurred over the course of the last time period. Have group members either break out into small groups or work with the whole group, depending on the size of the group and the ability of the group members to collaborate effectively.

4. *Offer appreciations.* This is an exercise developed by N. Kerth (2001) that can be used when needed. The facilitator asks the group for a volunteer who would like to express appreciation for another member of the group's efforts over the last time period. The person who receives the appreciation then selects someone whom he would like to thank, and the cycle continues until all individuals have both given and received appreciations. The coach will need to decide whether or not a group is ready for such an activity and whether or not it would be helpful. Cynics at senior levels may not "appreciate" such an exercise before it happens, but after it is over, they may find value in the bonding that can result.

5. *Identify action items.* Working from the timeline and their collective memory, the group members identify areas that need to be improved, sustained, or discussed further. These action items might include communication and feedback to other teams or adjustments in investment priorities and the project portfolio. Adjustments in the latter two areas will include the addition or modification of investment priorities, the addition of new project ideas, making improvements to projects that

are currently in the pipeline, or closing projects that are no longer necessary. Issues that require further discussion are also noted so that the group doesn't get bogged down for too long on issues that require additional data, time, or expertise to better understand.

Step 3d: Conduct the Retrospective

The retrospective is facilitated by the multi-level learning coach. As a skilled facilitator of learning and reflection, she helps team members look back on prior decisions in ways that limit defensive routines, reminding people about tools such as TALK, the Ladder of Inference, and collaborative conflict resolution techniques that focus on underlying needs rather than bargaining positions (see Chapter 3 for a detailed discussion of how and under what circumstances the coach should intervene to keep the group on track). When retrospectives are conducted more frequently, team members will become skilled in the art of asking questions in ways that lead to valid information, free and informed choice, and internal commitment. These ideals may seem daunting at first, especially with domineering and individualistic senior managers who are not accustomed to public reflection without the insinuation of blame or "finding the guilty." Yet because the facilitator strives for consensus on decisions, individual members can rely on the fact that they are collectively responsible for their decisions and, as a result, may be able to take joint responsibility for them.

The coach provides continual reminders of the principles of multi-level learning described in Chapter 2 so that the team is able to make the best use of its valuable resources, deliver results faster, focus on satisfying customers, and continuously learn and innovate at all three levels: project, process, and strategy. Questions to consider over the course of the retrospective include: Which projects and programs are required to enable us to achieve our intended strategy in the most cost-effective way? To what extent are the current projects moving us toward these objectives? What adjustments need to be made to ensure that we achieve our intended results? What actions need to be taken, and at which levels of the organization?

STEP 4: UPDATE THE PROJECT PORTFOLIO AND CAPTURE ACTION ITEMS

After the retrospective session, the PMO leader and coach work together to document the results and distribute them to team members. Follow-up meetings with subgroups or individuals may be required in order to take the actions determined in the meeting and to make adjustments to investment priorities and the project portfolio. Updates to the following documents may be required to ensure that the improvements are taken into the next iteration or time period:

- Action items
- Investment priorities
- The project portfolio (additions, revisions, and cancellations)
- The project dashboard
- Decision-making roles and responsibilities
- The benefits realization schedule
- Changes to the strategic intent statements
- Other "learning" that the team wants captured in the form of things to sustain or improve

The PMO leader works with team members to follow up on important improvements that need to be carried forward, including the decisions captured in the documents just listed. What matters most is that the team acts on the outcomes of the retrospective and that its members find the experience valuable. Therefore, it is good practice for the coach to facilitate feedback on the retrospective process itself, modeling the behavior of taking feedback and acting on it as appropriate, so that the team feels that it is being listened to and has an adequate degree of control over the group process and how it spends its time.

CONCLUSION

The goal of Level 3 of the multi-level learning approach is to provide a mechanism by which the senior management team can optimize the value of the organization's overall project portfolio by selecting and nurturing the right projects and programs at the right time with the right amount of resources. Consistent with the principles of multi-level learning, the senior management team reflects on ways to eliminate waste, deliver as fast as possible, and see the whole, while welcoming new insights, empowering team learning, using a third-party coach, and reflecting at three levels (project, process, and strategy).

Both the multi-level learning coach and the PMO play crucial roles in helping the senior team learn and adapt. Together, they improve the organization's ability to deliver on its strategic objectives by planning and conducting regular prospectives and retrospectives to ensure alignment between strategy and the overall project portfolio.

8 | CONCLUSION

When project organizations do not have effective mechanisms for improvement, learning remains largely informal and incidental. Improvement, innovation, and problem solving are often left to chance. Issues may go unaddressed or avoided, creating surprises, blowups, or "fire drills" that can occur abruptly, triggering a red light on the "traffic light" reporting system for project status. In these situations, project teams are hastily assembled so that senior managers can find out what went wrong, creating an environment that is riven by political infighting, personal threats to jobs and career prospects, "blamestorming," and avoidance of the "truth" for fear of reprisals by managers or peers. The result is that people at all levels actively avoid reflection, largely because it is perceived as being too threatening, political, ineffective, or all of the above. This creates a self-reinforcing cycle, because when structured reflection is avoided, the result is further opportunities for blowups and surprises.

Multi-level learning breaks this red-light learning cycle by providing organizations with a mechanism for continually improving results at each of the three levels: project, process, and strategy. The three levels of multi-level learning create a synergistic effect that enables teams at each level to build on the learning of the others, including project teams, program management teams, and senior management teams. This ensures that the right projects are selected at the right time, that project managers and teams are pooling their collective knowledge to streamline cross-project processes, and that project teams are continually innovating over the course of their work to improve project outcomes for customers and clients.

The multi-level learning coach facilitates improvement at each level through regular action-reflection cycles. The coach has no decision-making authority and serves as a substantively neutral third party who helps the organization overcome defensive routines that block learning.

The program management office (PMO) or program management function provides the "glue" for facilitating interlevel communication and feedback. As discussed at length in Chapter 4, the PMO leader serves the role of knowledge broker between the various communities of practice, providing coordination, translation, and alignment that connects their practices and embeds knowledge in the organization's processes, systems, methodologies, and tools to enable what Victoria Marsick and Karen Watkins (1999) call continuous systems-level learning. Because of the importance of the PMO leader's role, it is therefore essential that he be an effective knowledge broker. As discussed in Chapter 4, the leader needs legitimacy and social capital in order to have the influence required to facilitate continuous systems-level learning. This is not an easy role to play, yet it is an essential one if the organization is to learn from past failures, avoid repetition of mistakes, reduce waste, satisfy customers, and continually learn from experience.

Multi-level learning helps the organization reduce the risk of strategic failure, deliver projects and programs faster, make more efficient use of its scarce investment capital, satisfy customers, and create a more innovative, collaborative work environment for those involved. In this way, organizations can use multi-level learning to transform themselves so that they achieve higher levels of performance, significant competitive advantage, and success in reaching their strategic goals.

Sue Newell et al. (2006) claim that "we need to consider problems with the actual practice" of lessons learned. They claim that the fundamental problem with traditional codification practices—where knowledge is written and stored for future use—is the pervasive underlying assumption that knowledge can be possessed and therefore can be readily transferred to others in textual form. This view does not take into account the embedded, situated, and tacit nature of knowledge that manifests itself in practice. Newell et al. claim that "some knowledge can be possessed independently of practice . . . while other knowledge is deeply embedded in practice, making social networks necessary for knowledge sharing" (p. 170).

Ilan Oshri et al. (2006) demonstrate the negative impact of a "reuse" program designed with the cognitive "knowledge as possession" epistemology as its foundational structure. The researchers used an ethnographic case study approach to analyze a newly introduced knowledge-reuse program in the product development process of an Israeli defense product manufacturer. They found that management's efforts to reuse knowledge from past projects in product development had the unintended consequence of stifling the development of expertise. Before the reuse strategy was introduced, engineers and technicians developed unique, sometimes redundant designs, which led to "reinventing the wheel." Yet the motivation for learning and collaboration was high, and new engineers were developed through mentoring practices and exploratory learning opportunities.

The authors argue that it was the epistemological assumptions concerning how knowledge could be transferred between projects in the reuse strategy that created not only a problem in reusing knowledge across projects, but also a problem with fostering individual learning. According to the researchers, the change to a reuse strategy undervalued the situated nature of learning and knowledge sharing. The policy was for project teams to share design templates in knowledge-exchange meetings. However, the participants found it very difficult to transmit and incorporate a year's worth of problem solving through codified documents. Management undervalued the impact of social practices such as dialogue, storytelling, and problem solving on the effectiveness of transferring knowledge from project to project (Oshri et al., 2006).

Because of the ineffectiveness of the "knowledge as possession" model of knowledge exchange, Mike Bresnen et al. (2003) call for a "community-model" of sharing knowledge that "focuses instead upon the tacit dimension of knowledge and, in particular, its embeddedness or stickiness within particular social groupings" and "communities of practice." The community model "focuses on creating and maintaining the conditions required for the production of knowing. . . . Knowledge is context dependent since 'meanings' are interpreted in reference to a particular paradigm" (pp. 159–169). This model can be contrasted with the cognitive model, which focuses on the dissemination, imitation, and exploitation of knowledge, and which is the predominant epistemology underlying traditional lessons-learned approaches (Newell et al., 2006).

THE ROLE OF SOCIAL PRACTICES

Newell (2004) directly addresses the problem of reinventing the wheel on projects by selecting four projects from four different companies to demonstrate the challenges of cross-project learning. The findings provide further evidence of the limitations of traditional lessons-learned approaches involving codification and storage on databases. When project members did learn from experiences on other projects, this learning tended to occur through conversations with those in their personal networks whom they perceived as being able to help them with their particular problem. "The main finding was that people either relied on known acquaintances when seeking help or advice or solved the problems on their own through a process of trial and error or learning by doing" (p. 17).

Rather than investing in more intranet storage and retrieval systems, claim the authors, "managers need to think strategically about placing people on projects and organizing events that bring individuals from different projects together—not so much to specifically share learning and knowledge but to develop networks that can facilitate such sharing when the demand is activated by a particular project task" (p. 19).

In a study of the intra- and cross-project learning practices of 19 project-based organizations, Anne Keegan and J. Rodney Turner (2001) also found that informal networks were "the most important conduit for transferring learning between individuals and project teams." Indeed, after studying cross-project knowledge transfer in 13 unrelated projects across 6 U.K. organizations, Newell et al. (2006) suggest that effort put into social practices to facilitate cross-project learning "may be more effective than, or at least a necessary complement to, project documents and codified lessons learnt" (p. 180).

Further, in a study of two product development organizations, Marc Antoni et al. (2005) found that engineers considered "people-centered" vehicles to be more important than codification strategies for transferring improvement knowledge from project to project. Dialogical vehicles for transferring knowledge among people were found to include meetings, workshops with others who were working on similar projects, storytelling by mentors, and rotational staffing assignments across projects. And because postproject review practices are centered on the codification of lessons learned through a postproject report, the researchers found that "a reliance on post-project reviews to share knowledge across projects is doomed to fail, since this improvement structure is of low priority" (p. 890).

Further corroboration of these findings can be found in Andrea Prencipe and Frederick Tell's (2001) study of the mechanisms that organizations use to promote cross-project learning. They confirm that "the relationship between the sender and recipient in the knowledge transfer process is paramount [and that] integrative mechanisms, both formal and less formal, facilitate such learning" (p. 1391). Like Newell et al. (2006), the researchers suggest exploring community-based approaches to learning between projects, focusing on how various "communities of practice contribute to, or impair, more formal or technology-based initiatives" (Prencipe & Tell, p. 1391).

Likewise, in a study of five cases across project-based organizations in the United Kingdom, Bresnen et al. (2003) also found that the processes of knowledge capture, transfer, and learning across projects relied heavily upon "social patterns, practices and processes" among social networks and "communities of practice." In communities of practice, the authors explain, "Knowledge is constructed as individuals share ideas through collaborative mechanisms such as narration and joint work" (p. 161).

Karen Ayas (1996) draws on the assumptions of the social nature of situated, tacit knowledge as well as organizational learning theory to describe a structural approach to learning within and between projects. She proposes a network structure model of project organization that was developed, tested, and refined through action research with Fokker Aircraft. She claims that "professional" project management enables organizations "continually to enhance the underlying knowledge base—their learning capacity. This implies that all individuals involved in a project are engaged in a constant process of learning, that they transmit their learning to others and the cumulative knowledge acquired is then embodied in the project organization." The approach is based on the assumption that "continuous improvement in project management involves continuous learning." The project network structure model utilizes social networks as a means for making tacit knowledge explicit among team members on large, dispersed project teams. In subsequent research, Ayas claims that implementation of this approach, in conjunction with a number of other structured "reflective practices" conducted throughout the course of a project, made a tangible impact on reducing costs and cycle time for product development projects and encouraged the company to invest more in the development of its employees (Ayas & Zeniuk, 2001).

PROCESS VS. PRODUCT KNOWLEDGE

The importance of social practices is even more pronounced when organizations attempt to capture and transfer "process innovations" involving new work practices, roles, responsibilities, attitudes, or values (Bresnen et al., 2003).

Process innovations are a form of what Newell et al. (2006) consider to be "process knowledge." Process knowledge, in the context of cross-project learning, relates to processes that a team may have deployed to achieve its goals and includes the reasons why these processes were effective or why they were not. Process knowledge can be distinguished from "product knowledge," which the authors define as "knowledge about what had actually been achieved in relation to the stated goals or objectives" of a project (p. 175).

This account of the difference between product and process knowledge is consistent with Antoni et al. (2005), who describe product knowledge as technical, project-specific, and often well documented, whereas process knowledge tends to be more diffused in the organization, embedded in routines, and made up of a greater amount of undocumented, tacit knowledge.

Bresnen et al. (2003) claim that because process knowledge is developed over the course of a project and is often tacit, intangible, and context-dependent, it is more difficult to capture and apply. Product knowledge, on the other hand, can be more easily transferred in explicit forms through product design templates, diagrams, maps, and other artifacts.

Antoni et al. (2005) found that process knowledge was coded in the form of templates, checklists, manuals, and guidelines, and also found that these artifacts were put to use extensively, representing an accumulation of experience in managing product development projects. Project managers also maintained private diaries that included not only to-do lists, but notes about project occurrences such as how problem solving was conducted. Engineers considered these diaries to be very important in carrying individual learning from one project to the next.

Project Organization and the Dilemma of Process Knowledge

Traditional project management practice typically involves checkpoints to review "deliverables" produced by the project team for the purpose of meeting a project's specific objectives (Kerzner, 2006; Newell et al., 2006). Because project reviews and the completion of project work in general are highly focused on the production of deliverables, product knowledge, although potentially less useful, is what is stored in databases and most often is what is made available for sharing (Newell, 2004). Moreover, Antoni et al. (2005) find that product knowledge "enjoys higher status" than process knowledge among organizational members in their study.

Newell (2004) claims, however, that process knowledge, although more difficult to transfer, may be more useful to other project teams, as it "is likely to involve much less technical content and so will be easier for others to absorb." She goes on to say that "learning from [process knowledge] may enable a team in another project to complete their own tasks more efficiently and effectively" (p. 18). Similarly, Antoni et al. (2005) claim that process knowledge "can become a practice that can be applicable to most projects most of the time," whereas product knowledge "can vary significantly by application area" and is therefore less useful for a broader audience (p. 880).

The value and privilege associated with product knowledge, combined with the tendency to defer reflection about lessons learned until the end of projects—if reflection takes place at all—create significant barriers to improving upon previous project experiences. Newell et al. (2006) elaborate on this dilemma: "Things that the team had learned about and changed as they went along simply did not register as 'lessons learned' in post-project reviews because they had already been resolved. What was captured at the level of the project, then, was much more often 'product' knowledge rather than 'process' knowledge" (p. 175).

SUMMARY

Determining lessons learned has become standard in project management guidelines, yet the research is showing a very bleak state of affairs with respect to the deployment and efficacy of this material. Lessons learned are not always documented, and even when they are, they most often go unused (Antoni et al., 2005; Bresnen et al., 2003; Keegan & Turner, 2001; Newell, 2004; Newell et al., 2006; Prencipe & Tell, 2001). It is not surprising, then, that even though project management guidelines and internal company guidelines call for lessons learned to be completed at the end of projects, organizational members express clear dissatisfaction with the process (Keegan & Turner, 2001). Given the barriers identified, Newell et al. (2006) call for a consideration of the problems with the actual practice of lessons learned.

Two themes have emerged as factors that appear to enable cross-project learning. First, it is clear that social practices, including narration and joint work among communities of practitioners, appear to be more effective than technology-based approaches involving storage, access, and retrieval (Antoni et al., 2005; Bresnen et al., 2003; Newell, 2004; Newell et al., 2006; Newell & Swan, 2000; Prencipe & Tell, 2001). Even where technology is involved, organizational members tend to consult with trusted colleagues first in order to identify information that may be useful (Bresnen et al., 2003; Newell et al., 2006).

The second factor emerging from this literature is the conceptual difference between process knowledge and product knowledge. Although it is potentially more difficult to transfer because of its tacit, intangible, and context-dependent nature, process knowledge may be more valuable for cross-project learning because of its broader applicability by other project members. This is in contrast to product knowledge, which tends to be more technical and project-specific (Antoni et al., 2005; Bresnen et al., 2003; Bresnen et al., 2005; Newell, 2004; Newell et al., 2006; Zedtwitz, 2002).

APPENDIX B:
SITUATED LEARNING AND
COMMUNITIES OF PRACTICE

Previous research related to cross-project learning has been reviewed in order to understand what organizations have attempted to do to foster cross-project learning and to identify the barriers and enablers associated with these efforts. The cross-project learning literature has pointed to the need to adopt a situated learning approach that takes into account the socially embedded nature of knowledge and its development within communities of practice.

This section begins with a review of J. Lave and E. Wenger's (1991) original work on situated learning and legitimate peripheral participation. The review then turns to Wenger's (1998) subsequent work in further elaborating the role of "communities of practice" and how they shape learning among shared work practitioners in organizations.

SITUATED LEARNING AND
LEGITIMATE PERIPHERAL PARTICIPATION

Situated learning and communities of practice have been proposed as fertile ground for further empirical research on cross-project learning (Ayas & Zeniuk, 2001; Kotnour, 2000). Situated learning is founded on the assumption that learning is inherently social and that tools, social activities, and social context shape it (Hansman, 2001).

In *Situated Learning: Legitimate Peripheral Participation*, Lave and Wenger (1991) argue against a view of learning that focuses on individuals' acquiring, internalizing, and transferring knowledge. This traditional view, manifested in schools and classrooms, ignores the fundamentally human issues of meaning and identity and their interconnectedness with the social world in which we live our everyday lives. Lave and Wenger posit an alternative view that locates learning within everyday social contexts, taking place as an aspect of social participation. The theory of legitimate peripheral participation was derived from Lave's studies of craft apprenticeship and was strongly influenced by Marxist theories of social practice, particularly P. Bourdieu's (1977) social activity theory. The authors describe the development of their theory as a three-stage process: (1) from learning as apprenticeship to (2) the concept of situated learning to (3) the concept of legitimate peripheral participation.

Apprenticeship

Lave and Wenger originally found apprenticeship to be a particularly useful phenomenon for understanding learning. Apprentices develop expertise without the traditional forms of instruction associated with schools, teachers, and examinations. Apprenticeship does not involve lesson plans and formal curricula. Instead, the "curriculum" of apprenticeship provides the apprentice with opportunities for observation and participation in ongoing work practices as a way to develop expertise. Motivation emerges from developing competence and contributing to practices that are valued.

Through ethnographic studies of Vai and Gola tailors in Liberia, quartermasters in the U.S. Navy, midwives in the Yucatan, butchers in U.S. supermarkets, and nondrinking alcoholics in Alcoholics Anonymous, Lave and Wenger found concrete examples of how work and learning are seamlessly related and how they shape identity, motivation, and meaning within specific social structures.

Importantly, the authors draw on H. Becker's (1972) work to highlight the "disastrous possibilities that structural constraints in work organizations may curtail or extinguish apprentices' access to the full range of activities of the job, and hence to possibilities for learning what they need to know to master a trade" (Lave & Wenger, p. 86). This was evident from the study of U.S. butchers, who sequestered their apprentices in separate physical spaces, disabling their capacity to learn from the "masters."

Situated Learning

In addition to building on their and others' studies of apprenticeship, Lave and Wenger report that their theory also emerged out of the need to overcome confusion over what was meant by "situated learning." They identify a number of conceptions of situated learning with which they disagree. The first conception of situated learning that the authors reject is one that simply locates learners in a particular setting. This simplistic notion fails to explain why the particular setting matters for the learner. The second notion is that learning simply takes place within a social context. This is also inadequate in its explanation of the relationship of the social context to learning. A third notion, in which situated learning is seen as being synonymous with "learning by doing" outside of traditional school contexts, fails to locate schools as specific contexts themselves. As Lave later explains, all learning is in context. "Decontextualized learning" is a contradiction in terms (Lave, 1993).

A final notion of situated learning that Lave and Wenger reject is one that sees learning as always being specific to a given time or task. The authors agree that learning is sometimes limited to specific situations. However, they argue that general knowledge can also emanate from specific situations. Stories, for example, are concrete understandings that can relate to a specific context, yet can also be applied in other practice settings. The authors believe, therefore, that knowledge can be transferable from one situation, setting, or context to another, although this may not always be the case.

For Lave and Wenger, the development of a theory of situated learning became more complex than these interpretations. Their conception viewed situated learning as "the basis of claims about the relational character of knowledge and learning, about the negotiated character of meaning, and about the concerned (engaged, dilemma-driven) nature of learning activity for the people involved." In this view, "agent, activity and the world mutually constitute each other" (p. 33).

This view is consistent with C. A. Hansman (2001), who describes situated learning as "people learning as they participate and become intimately involved with a community or culture of learning, interacting with the community and learning to understand and participate in its history, assumptions and cultural values and rules" (p. 45).

Legitimate Peripheral Participation

Lave and Wenger's view of situated learning served as a transition from viewing learning as a cognitive process to viewing learning as an inseparable aspect of social practice. Their notion of situated learning was a bridge to the development of a "specific analytic approach to learning" (p. 35) that they called *legitimate peripheral participation*. This evolution in their thinking highlights *how* people learn as they take action within communities of practice. Mastery of knowledge and skill is achieved when newcomers to the community move toward full participation in the practices engaged in by that community. Legitimacy depends on whether or not a newcomer's participation is sanctioned by the community. As Wenger (1998) states, legitimacy can take many forms, including "being useful, being sponsored, being feared, being the right kind of person, having the right birth" (p. 101).

Legitimate peripheral participation "suggests that there are multiple, varied, more- or less-engaged and inclusive ways of being located in the fields of participation defined by a community" (p. 36).

COMMUNITIES OF PRACTICE

Etienne Wenger, Richard McDermott, and William Snyder (2002) define communities of practice as "groups of people who share a concern, a set of problems, or a passion about a topic, and who deepen their knowledge and expertise in this area by interacting on an ongoing basis." They observe that communities of practice are "in the best position to codify knowledge, because they can combine its tacit and explicit aspects" (pp. 4–9).

In *Communities of Practice: Learning, Meaning, and Identity*, Wenger (1998) expounds on the concept of communities of practice to further develop a social theory of learning. In this expanded account, practice is seen as an element of four key dimensions of Wenger's theory: as the basis for the social production of meaning, as the source of coherence in a community, as a learning process, and as the source of boundaries between interlinked communities at both the local and the societal levels. Each of Wenger's dimensions of practice will now be described in relation to how PMO leaders might learn from project successes and failures within their organization.

Practice as the Basis for the Production of Meaning

Through practice, our lives become meaningful (Wenger, 1998). As Wenger claims, "Whether we are talking, acting, thinking, solving problems, or daydreaming, we are concerned with meanings" (p. 53). As we live our lives, we are constantly undergoing the process of negotiating meaning. We are linked to the history of our communities by the structures and ways of being that have previously been established, yet we are not bound by them. We are able to negotiate new meaning through the convergence of two processes that continually interact with each other: participation and reification. These processes form a duality that is "fundamental to the negotiation of meaning." *Participation* refers to our interactions with others and our ongoing activities as we live and work. The concept of participation is meant to convey the "profoundly social character of our experience of life."

Reification, the other half of the duality through which we negotiate meaning, refers to the "process of giving form to our experience by producing objects that congeal this experience into 'thingness.'" The process of reification "produces abstractions, tools, symbols, stories, terms, and concepts that reify something of that practice in a congealed form" (pp. 58–59). It is through the process of reification that forms can "take a life of their own, beyond their context of origin." This account is consistent with Newell et al.'s (2006) claim that "some knowledge can be possessed independently of practice . . . while other knowledge is deeply embedded in practice, making social networks necessary for knowledge sharing" (p. 170).

In this view, we would expect to see PMO leaders engaged in forms of social participation that involve tools, stories, and templates to conduct their work.

Practice as the Source of Community Coherence

Through practice, communities develop coherence. Wenger (1998) defines three characteristics of practice that relate to community coherence. The first is mutual engagement. Practice exists because community members engage in actions through which they negotiate meaning. Membership in a community of practice is based upon mutual engagement.

The second characteristic of practice that relates to community coherence is joint enterprise. Joint enterprise goes beyond stated goals such as mission statements or objectives. It is defined and continuously renegotiated by participants as they respond to their situation. Joint enterprise is what creates mutual accountability among community members. It is a "resource of coordination, of sense-making, of mutual engagement; it is like rhythm to music" (p. 82). Claims processing is an example of a joint enterprise through which claims processors engage one another in a shared practice.

The third dimension of practice that creates community coherence is a shared repertoire. Over time, Wenger claims, "the joint pursuit of an enterprise creates resources for negotiating meaning." These resources are products of the previously described interplay of reification and participation processes through which members negotiate meaning. They include "routines, words, tools, ways of doing things, stories, gestures, symbols . . . that the community has produced or adopted in the course of its existence, and which have become part of its practice" (pp. 82–83).

The combination of these three dimensions of community coherence—mutual engagement, joint enterprise, and shared repertoire—has the potential to create a "social energy" that binds community members. The social energy generated by the community can, on the one hand, "give rise to an experience of meaningfulness" and, on the other hand, "hold us hostages to that experience" (p. 85). As Wenger states:

> The local coherence of a community of practice can be both a strength and a weakness. The indigenous production of practice makes communities of practice the locus of creative achievements and the locus of inbred failures; the locus of resistance to oppression and the locus of the reproduction of its conditions; the cradle of the self but also the potential cage of the soul. (p. 85)

Practice as a Learning Process

Through practice, communities also learn. With time and sustained mutual engagement in a joint enterprise, the interplay of participation and reification produces what Wenger calls a "shared history of learning." Reification "yields a memory of forms that allows our engagement in practice to leave enduring imprints in the world." Participation, on the other hand, affords opportunities for collecting individual memories. It is through participation that we become who we are—how we fashion our identities—and "recognize ourselves in our past" (p. 88). The products of reification and participation thus create a shared history of learning that is manifested in the world through shared language, stories, physical objects, and memories. The resulting history of shared learning that is created is a source of learning for newcomers to the community as they engage in legitimate peripheral participation (Lave & Wenger, 1991).

Because of their residual historical effects, reification and participation offer two paths for community members in their attempts to shape the future: "1) You can seek, cultivate, or avoid specific relationships with specific people. 2) You can produce or promote specific artifacts to focus future negotiation of meaning in specific ways" (Wenger, 1998, p. 91). Because of their ability to shape collective history and the agency this affords for community members, participation and reification are distinct channels of power. Thus, Wenger describes a distinct form of politics associated with each of them. "The politics of participation includes influence, personal authority, nepotism, rampant discrimination, charisma, trust, friendship, ambition. . . . Of a different nature are the politics of reification, which include legislation, policies, institutionally defined authority, expositions, argumentative demonstrations, statistics, contracts, plans, designs" (p. 92).

As members come and go, as the world changes, and as participants attempt to shape shared practices in these ways, learning takes place and the community's history is renegotiated. For Wenger, all learning takes place within the context of communities that share a history, are mutually engaged, have a joint enterprise, and have a shared repertoire. And it is along these dimensions that learning is manifested:

- *Forms of mutual engagement evolve.* These include "discovering how to engage, what helps and what hinders; developing mutual relationships;

defining identities, establishing who is who, who is good at what, who knows what, who is easy or hard to get along with."

- *Joint enterprise is renegotiated and tuned by the community.* This includes "aligning their engagement with it, and learning to become and hold each other accountable to it; struggling to define the enterprise and reconciling conflicting interpretations of what the enterprise is about."
- *Shared repertoire is developed and refined.* This includes "renegotiating the meaning of various elements; producing or adopting tools, artifacts, representations; recording and recalling events; inventing new terms and redefining or abandoning old ones; telling and retelling stories; creating and breaking routines" (p. 95).

Practice as the Source of Boundaries Between Interlinked Communities

Through practice, boundaries are created between communities. Economies, countries, organizations, and even neighborhoods consist of a multitude of communities of practice. Wenger claims that these larger units of analysis can be viewed as a "constellation" of interconnected practices. Shared histories of learning in a community also include articulations of how a community engages those who are external to it. Yet shared histories not only create discontinuities across boundaries, but can also create continuities across boundaries through "boundary objects" and "brokering."

Boundary objects are products of reification—artifacts, documents, terms, concepts, or stories—that organize interconnections among communities. To the extent that the products of reification belong to multiple practices, "they are a nexus of perspectives and thus carry the potential of becoming boundary objects if those perspectives need to be coordinated" (p. 107). Reading a memo that is a boundary object, for example, is not just a relationship between the person and the memo, but a relationship between the person and two or more communities of practice.

Brokering is the process of establishing connections between communities by "introducing elements of one practice into another" (p. 105). Project managers leading cross-functional projects, for example, may belong to a community of project management professionals associated with a PMO as well as to a community of engineers within which their career has progressed. Likewise, PMO leaders themselves might participate in a community of project management professionals while engaging managers and business leaders responsible for running a business unit. Both the project manager and the PMO leader in this case have the potential to broker new connections between practices, and "if they are good brokers—open new possibilities for meaning" (p. 109).

DeFillippi (2001) supports the learning potential of brokering roles by suggesting that it may be possible that "the deepest learning accrues to people who assume brokering roles at the intersections of multiple communities engaged in projects requiring joint cooperation among their contributors" (p. 6).

M. T. Hansen's (1999) study of network ties in 41 divisions of a large R&D organization also reinforces the importance of brokers who can span multiple communities of practice. She sought to understand more about how the strength of social network "ties" between organizational units affected the units' ability to share knowledge. Consistent with Wenger's communities of practice, strong ties between units, characterized by "close and frequent interactions," were found to be more important when the knowledge is highly complex, noncodified, and dependent. Weak ties, on the other hand, characterized by "distant and infrequent interactions," were more important for knowledge-sharing when the knowledge was noncomplex, highly codified, and less dependent on context, supporting the key role of brokers and boundary spanners in knowledge-exchange processes.

The Challenges of Brokering. Wenger (1998) characterizes brokering as a complex process that involves translation, coordination, and alignment among perspectives. He elaborates further on the role and competencies required of brokers if they are to facilitate learning:

> It requires enough legitimacy to influence the development of a practice, mobilize attention, and address conflicting interests. It also requires the ability to link practices by facilitating transactions between them, and to cause learning by introducing into a practice elements of another. (p. 109)

Because boundaries lack the negotiated understanding of what defines competence at full participation in a community of practice, the value of brokering can be difficult to recognize. As a result, "brokers sometimes interpret the uprootedness associated with brokering in personal terms of individual adequacy." Brokering, therefore, requires an ability to "manage carefully the coexistence of membership and non-membership, yielding enough distance to bring a different perspective, but also enough legitimacy to be listened to" (p. 110).

Boundary Encounters. Wenger describes three types of "boundary encounters," defined as "single or discrete events that provide connections" across practices. The first type of boundary encounter is a one-on-one meeting, where conversations between two "interlocutors" allow private matters to be discussed in more candid ways. The downside of this type of encounter is that the connection created is "hostage to the partiality of each interlocutor" (pp. 112–113). That is because no single member of either community could be fully representative of her community's practices, nor is her memory capable of covering such ground with perfection. Moreover, in isolation, single members cannot fully act as they would when they are participating in the milieu of everyday practice.

The second type of boundary encounter is immersion in a practice by visiting the site at which the activity takes place. This provides a more comprehensive perspective on the practices of the host and how members engage one another. The downside of this approach is that the connection is one-way: The host is unlikely to learn much about how visitors function in the host's environment.

The third type of boundary encounter involves delegations from each practice meeting simultaneously. There are two advantages to this approach. First, the negotiation (of meaning) process can occur within and across the delegations at the same time. Second, the process allows each community to see how the other negotiates meaning. The downside of delegation encounters is that "participants may cling to their own internal relations, perspectives, and ways of thinking."

Boundary Practices. If boundary encounters become an ongoing forum for mutual engagement across practice boundaries, Wenger claims, a practice is likely to start emerging, particularly if delegations are involved. The enterprise of the boundary practice is to "sustain a connection between a number of other practices by addressing conflicts, reconciling perspectives, and finding resolutions" (p. 114). The resulting practice becomes a form of "collective brokering." As with practice in general, the interplay of participation and reification helps participants negotiate meaning and overcome the problems associated with isolated boundary objects or brokers, either of which can inhibit meaning-making.

Project Environments and Communities of Practice

Ayas and Zeniuk (2001) claim that communities of practice in project-based organizations offer an "excellent opportunity to engage in learning" at the individual, organizational, and societal levels. They suggest that temporary membership on project teams enables the members of those teams to engage in multiple communities of practice and to build and cultivate relationships over the course of their work within and across projects. Multimembership in communities of practice, claim the authors, contributes to "creating informal webs of people who act as knowledge brokers" across practice boundaries (p. 71). They go on to argue that:

> Project-based organizations may grow into constellations of inter-related communities of practice, offering a web of mutual support for cultivating reflective practices. When projects share members, they are bound together and become embedded in the same social network. The recursive interaction among projects creates social networks of mutual assistance. (p. 72)

Through four case studies and reflective workshops with members from 20 projects in separate companies, M. B. Arthur et al. (2001) also found communities of practice to be an important mechanism for promoting project-based learning within and between projects. By nurturing communities of practice, they claim, organizations can provide access to knowledge among community members that can "endure after formal project-based activities cease," providing a "continuing source of new information, wherever the project members are presently located" (p. 113).

Limitations of Communities of Practice in Relation to Cross-Project Learning

Although communities of practice offer a lens into how PMO leaders might negotiate and share project lessons learned, two inhibiting factors of communities of practice in relation to cross-project learning merit consideration. The first limitation is identified by Wenger (1998), who recognizes that as communities develop greater coherence, their boundaries with "outsiders" may become stronger, and this may inhibit the introduction of new knowledge into their practice. In a comparative case study of two construction projects, H. Scarbrough et al. (2004) conclude that as deeper and unique knowledge is developed at the project level through shared practice, it is exactly this new division of practice between the project and the permanent organization that makes it more difficult to transfer the knowledge to others.

The second limitation of communities of practice with respect to cross-project learning relates to the nature of the learning that takes place among practitioners (Lave & Wenger, 1991). Marsick (2000) characterizes situated learning and legitimate peripheral participation as phenomena in which learning "may be tacit or not highly conscious . . . and acquired primarily through trial and error, observation, modeling and socialization." The tacit nature of the learning that results can "dilute or distort lessons learned," preventing practitioners from fully understanding the reasons for success and failure (p. 12). Therefore, the informal and incidental nature of the learning that takes place within communities of practice underscores the need for structured reflective practices that focus on improving future actions (Marsick & Watkins, 1999; Raelin, 2001; Roth & Kleiner, 1998).

REFERENCES

Antoni, M., L. Nilsson-Witell, and J. J. Dahlgaard (2005). "Inter-Project Improvement in Product Development." *International Journal of Quality & Reliability Management*, 22(8 / 9), 876.

Argyris, C. (1990). *Overcoming Organizational Defenses: Facilitating Organizational Learning*. Wellesley, Mass.: Prentice Hall Professional Technical Reference.

Argyris, C. (1995). "Action Science and Organizational Learning." *Journal of Managerial Psychology*, 10(6), 20.

Argyris, C., and D. A. Schön (1978). *Organizational Learning*. Reading, Mass.: Addison-Wesley.

Argyris, C., and D. Schön (1996). *Organizational Learning II: Theory, Method, and Practice*. Reading, Mass.: Addison-Wesley.

Arthur, M. B., R. J. DeFillippi, and C. Jones (2001). "Project-Based Learning as the Interplay of Career and Company Non-financial Capital." *Management Learning*, 32(1), 99.

Ayas, K. (1996). "Professional Project Management: A Shift Towards Learning and a Knowledge Creating Structure." *International Journal of Project Management*, 14, 133–136.

Ayas, K., and N. Zeniuk (2001). "Project-Based Learning: Building Communities of Reflective Practitioners." *Management Learning*, 32(1), 61.

Beck, K., M. Beedle, A. v. Bennekum, A. Cockburn, W. Cunningham, M. Fowler, et al. (2001). The Agile Manifesto; from www.agilemanifesto.org.

Becker, H. (1972). "A School Is a Lousy Place to Learn Anything In." *American Behavioral Scientist*, 16, 85–105.

Becker, M. C. (2004) "Organizational Routines: A Review of the Literature." *Industrial and Corporate Change*, 13(4), 643.

Becker, M. C. (2005). "A Framework for Applying Organizational Routines in Empirical Research: Linking Antecedents, Characteristics and Performance Outcomes of Recurrent Interaction Patterns." *Industrial and Corporate Change*, 14(5), 817.

191

Becker, M. C., N. Lazaric, R. R. Nelson, and S. G. Winter (2005). "Applying Organizational Routines in Understanding Organizational Change." *Industrial and Corporate Change*, 14(5), 775.

Berlew, D. (1993). "Teams and the Importance of Goals." *Quality Digest*, 34.

Bourdieu, P. (1977). *Outline of a Theory of Practice*. Cambridge, U.K.; New York: Cambridge University Press.

Bresnen, M., L. Edelman, S. Newell, H. Scarbrough, and J. Swan (2003). "Social Practices and the Management of Knowledge in Project Environments." *International Journal of Project Management*, 21(3), 157.

Bresnen, M., A. Goussevskaia, and J. Swan (2005). "Organizational Routines, Situated Learning and Processes of Change in Project-Based Organizations." *Project Management Journal*, 36(3), 27.

Cervero, R. W., and A. Wilson. (2001). "At the Heart of Practice: The Struggle for Knowledge and Power." In R. W. Cervero and A.Wilson (eds.), *Power in Practice: Adult Education and the Struggle for Knowledge and Power in Society* (pp. 1–20). San Francisco: Jossey-Bass.

Cressey, P., D. Boud, and P. Docherty (2006). *The Emergence of Productive Reflection*. New York: Routledge.

Dai, C. X. (2002). *The Role of the Project Management Office in Achieving Project Success*. Unpublished 3034791, George Washington University, Washington, D.C.

Dai, C. X., and W. G. Wells (2004). "An Exploration of Project Management Office Features and Their Relationship to Project Performance." *International Journal of Project Management*, 22(7), 523.

Darling, M., C. Parry, and J. Moore (2005). "Learning in the Thick of It." *Harvard Business Review*, 83(7), 84.

DeFillippi, R. J. (2001). "Introduction: Project-Based Learning, Reflective Practices and Learning Outcomes." *Management Learning*, 32(1), 5.

DeFillippi, R. J., and M. B. Arthur (1998). "Paradox in Project-Based Enterprise: The Case of Film Making." *California Management Review*, 40(2), 125.

DeJong, J. (2006). "At the Five-Year Mark, Agile Manifesto Still Stands." *Software Development Times* (146), 1.

Derby, E., and D. Larsen (2006). *Agile Retrospectives: Making Good Teams Great*. Raleigh, N.C.: Pragmatic Bookshelf.

Disterer, G. (2002). "Management of Project Knowledge and Experiences." *Journal of Knowledge Management*, 6(5), 512.

Ekstedt, E. (1999). *Neo-Industrial Organising Renewal by Action and Knowledge Formation in a Project-Intensive Economy*. London; New York: Routledge.

Engle, P. (2005). "The Project Management Office." *Industrial Engineer*, 37(1), 20.

Feldman, M. S., and B. T. Pentland (2003). "Reconceptualizing Organizational Routines as a Source of Flexibility and Change." *Administrative Science Quarterly*, 48(1), 94.

Fisher, R., and W. Ury (1991). *Getting to Yes*. Boston: Penguin Group.

Gulliver, F. R. (1987). "Post-Project Appraisals Pay." *Harvard Business Review*, 65(2), 128.

Hansen, M. T. (1999). "The Search-Transfer Problem: The Role of Weak Ties in Sharing Knowledge Across Organization Subunits." *Administrative Science Quarterly*, 44(1), 82.

Hansman, C. A. (2001). "Context-Based Adult Learning." In S. Merriam (ed.), *The New Update on Adult Learning Theory* (pp. 45ff.). San Francisco: Jossey-Bass.

Highsmith, J. (1999). *Adaptive Software Development: A Collaborative Approach to Managing Complex Systems*. New York: Dorset House Publishing.

Julian, J. (2008a). "How Project Management Office Leaders Facilitate Cross-Project Learning and Continuous Improvement." *Project Management Journal*, 39(3), 43–58.

Julian, J. (2008b). "How Knowledge Management Professionals Can Improve Cross-Project Learning in Project-Based Organizations." *KMPro Journal*, 5(2), 6–13.

Julian, J. (2008c). "An Exploratory Study of How Project Management Office Leaders Facilitate Cross-Project Learning and Continuous Improvement." Ed.D. diss., Columbia University, New York City.

Keegan, A., and J. R. Turner (2001). "Quantity Versus Quality in Project-Based Learning Practices." *Management Learning*, 32(1), 77.

Kilmann, R., and K. Thomas (1977). "Developing a Forced-Choice Measure of Conflict-Handling Behavior: The 'Mode' Instrument." *Educational and Psychological Measurement*, 37(2), 309–325.

Kerth, N. (2001). *Project Retrospectives: A Handbook for Team Reviews*. New York: Dorset House Publishing.

Kerzner, H. (2004). *Advanced Project Management: Best Practices on Implementation*, 2nd ed. Hoboken, N.J.: John Wiley & Sons.

Kerzner, H. (2006). *Project Management Best Practices: Achieving Global Excellence*. Hoboken, N.J.: John Wiley & Sons.

Kotnour, T. (2000). "Organizational Learning Practices in the Project Management Environment." *International Journal of Quality & Reliability Management*, 17 (4/5), 393.

Kotnour, T., and C. Vergopia (2005). "Learning-Based Project Reviews: Observations and Lessons Learned from the Kennedy Space Center." *Engineering Management Journal*, 17(4), 30.

Lave, J. (1993). "The Practice of Learning." In S. Chaiklin and J. Lave (eds.), *Understanding Practice: Perspectives on Activity and Context* (pp. x, 414). Cambridge, U.K.; New York: Cambridge University Press.

Lave, J., and E. Wenger (1991). *Situated Learning: Legitimate Peripheral Participation*. Cambridge, U.K.; New York: Cambridge University Press.

Lavell, D., and R. Martinelli (2008a). "Program and Project Retrospectives: A Success Story of Three Teams." *PM World Today*, X, 1–5.

Lavell, D., and R. Martinelli (2008b). "Program and Project Retrospectives: Achieving Organizational Buy-In." *PM World Today*, X.

Lavell, D., and R. Martinelli (2008c). "Program and Project Retrospectives: An Introduction." *PM World Today*, X, 1–5.

Marsick, V. (2000). "Learning Organizations." In V. Marsick, J. Bitterman, and R. Van der Veen (eds.), *From the Learning Organization to Learning Communities Toward a*

Learning Society (pp. 5–19). Columbus, Ohio: ERIC Clearinghouse on Adult, Career, and Vocational Education.

Marsick, V., and K. Watkins (1999). *Facilitating Learning Organizations: Making Learning Count*. Hampshire, U.K.: Gower.

Marsick, V., and K. Watkins (2001). "Informal and Incidental Learning." *New Directions for Adult and Continuing Education*, 2001 (89), 25–34.

Mezirow, J. (1991). *Transformative Dimensions of Adult Learning*. San Francisco: Jossey-Bass.

Nahapiet, J., and S. Ghoshal (1998). "Social Capital, Intellectual Capital, and the Organizational Advantage." *Academy of Management Review*, 23(2), 242.

Newell, S. (2004). "Enhancing Cross-Project Learning." *Engineering Management Journal*, 16(1), 12.

Newell, S., and J. Swan (2000). "Trust and Inter-Organizational Networking." *Human Relations*, 53(10), 1287.

Newell, S., M. Bresnen, L. Edelman, H. Scarbrough, and J. Swan (2006). "Sharing Knowledge Across Projects: Limits to ICT-Led Project Review Practices." *Management Learning*, 37, 167–185.

O'Neil, J., and V. Marsick (2007). *Understanding Action Learning*. New York: AMACOM.

Oshri, I., S. L. Pan, and S. Newell (2006). "Managing Trade-offs and Tensions Between Knowledge Management Initiatives and Expertise Development Practices." *Management Learning*, 37(1), 63.

Polanyi, M. (1967). *The Tacit Dimension*. Garden City, N.Y.: Doubleday.

Poppendieck, M., and T. Poppendieck (2003). *Lean Software Development: An Agile Toolkit*. Boston: Addison-Wesley.

Prencipe, A., and F. Tell (2001). "Inter-Project Learning: Processes and Outcomes of Knowledge Codification in Project-Based Firms." *Research Policy*, 30(9), 1373.

Project Management Institute (2004). *A Guide to the Project Management Body of Knowledge*. Newtown Square, Pa.: Project Management Institute.

Rad, P., and G. Levin (2002). *The Advanced Project Management Office: A Comprehensive Look at Function and Implementation*. Boca Raton, Fla.: St. Lucie Press.

Raelin, J. A. (2001). "Public Reflection as the Basis of Learning." *Management Learning*, 32(1), 11.

Raider, E., S. Coleman, and J. Gerson (2006). "Teaching Conflict Resolution Skills in a Workshop." In Morton Deutsch, Peter T. Coleman, and Eric C. Marcus (eds.), *The Handbook of Conflict Resolution: Theory and Practice*, 2nd ed. San Francisco: Jossey-Bass.

Revans, R. W. (1971). *Developing Effective Managers: A New Approach to Business Education*. New York: Praeger Publishers.

Roth, G., and A. Kleiner (1998). "Developing Organizational Memory Through Learning Histories." *Organizational Dynamics*, 27(2), 43.

Rubin, I., M. Plovnick, and R. Fry (1975). *Task-Oriented Team Development*. New York: McGraw-Hill.

Rubin, J., D. G. Pruitt, and S. H. Kim (1994). *Social Conflict Escalation: Stalemate and Settlement.* New York: McGraw-Hill.

Scarbrough, H., J. Swan, S. Laurent, and M. Bresnen (2004). "Project-Based Learning and the Role of Learning Boundaries." *Organization Studies,* 25(9), 1579.

Schein, E. (1999). *Process Consultation Revisited: Building the Helping Relationship.* Reading, Mass.: Addison-Wesley.

Schindler, M., and M. J. Eppler (2003). "Harvesting Project Knowledge: A Review of Project Learning Methods and Success Factors." *International Journal of Project Management,* 21(3), 219.

Schön, D. A. (1990). *Educating the Reflective Practitioner.* San Francisco: Jossey-Bass.

Schwaber, K. (2004). *Agile Project Management with SCRUM.* Redmond, Wash.: Microsoft.

Schwarz, R. (1994). *The Skilled Facilitator: Practical Wisdom for Developing Effective Groups.* San Francisco: Jossey-Bass.

Schwarz, R. (2002). *The Skilled Facilitator: Practical Wisdom for Developing Effective Groups,* rev. ed. San Francisco: Jossey-Bass.

Senge, P. (2006). *The Fifth Discipline: The Art and Practice of the Learning Organization.* New York: Doubleday.

Stanleigh, M. (2006). "From Crisis to Control: New Standards for Project Management." *Ivey Business Journal Online,* 1.

Szulanski, G., and R. J. Jensen (2004). "Overcoming Stickiness: An Empirical Investigation of the Role of the Template in the Replication of Organizational Routines." *Managerial and Decision Economics,* 25(6–7), 347.

Takeuchi, H., and I. O. Nonaka (1986). "The New Product Development Game." *Harvard Business Review* (January 1986), 64(1), 137–146.

Walker, D. H. T., and D. Christenson (2005). "Knowledge Wisdom and Networks: A Project Management Centre of Excellence Example." *Learning Organization,* 12(3), 275.

Wenger, E. (1998). *Communities of Practice: Learning, Meaning, and Identity.* Cambridge, U.K.: Cambridge University Press.

Wenger, E., R. A. McDermott, and W. Snyder (2002). *Cultivating Communities of Practice: A Guide to Managing Knowledge.* Boston: Harvard Business School Press.

Zedtwitz, M. v. (2002). "Organizational Learning Through Post-Project Reviews in R&D." *R & D Management,* 32(3), 255.

Zedtwitz, M. v. (2003). "Post-Project Reviews in R&D." *Research Technology Management,* 46(5), 43.

Zollo, M., and S. G. Winter (2002). "Deliberate Learning and the Evolution of Dynamic Capabilities." *Organization Science,* 13(3), 339.

INDEX

accommodating style, in conflict resolution, 63–64

accountability, 40

action items, in strategic portfolio alignment, 165, 166–167

action learning research, 22, 29

action-reflection cycles, 34, 45–47, 169–170

Adaptive Software Development, 35

AEIOU mnemonic, in conflict resolution, 65

After Action Review (AAR; U.S. Army), 27, 40

    action-reflection cycles in, 34

    before-action planning in, 30, 31

    facilitation of, 30

    importance of reflection and, 30–31

    questions addressed in, 30–31

Agile Manifesto (Beck et al.), 32

agile software development, 31–33

    action-reflection cycles and, 34

    advantages of, 33

    extent of use, 31

    impact of, 33

    methodology of, 32–33

    nature of, 2, 32

    principles of multi-level learning and, 35–40

    Scrum and, 32–33

    "waterfall" approach versus, 32, 36–37, 139, 162

alignment

    in brokering role, 66, 77–78, 82–83, 152

    see also strategic portfolio alignment

annual performance objectives, in strategic portfolio alignment, 154

Antoni, Marc, 22, 116, 173, 175–177

appreciations

    in continuous project improvement, 134

    in strategic portfolio alignment, 165

apprenticeship, 179–180

Argyris, Chris, 19, 25–26, 51, 54, 56–57, 59, 74, 112

Arthur, M. B., 114, 188

artifacts

    in continuous project improvement, 133

    in strategic portfolio alignment, 165

attacking behaviors, in conflict resolution, 65

avoidance mechanisms, 19–21, 39

avoiding style, in conflict resolution, 63–64

Ayas, Karen, 174, 178, 188

barriers to cross-project improvement, 98, 103–109

    changes in project personnel, 49–50, 70–71, 105–106

    fear of publicly airing mistakes, 106–107

    lack of access to past lessons learned, 109

    lack of direct authority, 103–104, 110

CPSIA information can be obtained
at www.ICGtesting.com
Printed in the USA
JSHW030016240323
39350JS00008B/84